ALIVE

DIGITAL HUMANS AND THEIR ORGANIZATIONS

Alive: digital humans and their organizations

Published by Novaro Publishing Ltd, Techno Park, Coventry University Technology Park, Puma Way, Coventry CV1 2TT

ISBN 978-1-9998329-2-6

British Library Cataloguing in Publication Data
A catalogue record for this book is available from the British Library.

Cover designed by Lawston Design.
Typeset by Ravina Patel.
Printed and bound in Great Britain by Marston Book Services Ltd, Oxfordshire

ALIVE

DIGITAL HUMANS AND THEIR ORGANIZATIONS

PAUL ASHCROFT
GARRICK JONES

NOVARO PUBLISHING

For Zsanett, Benjamin, Leanne, Georgia, Leila and Emma

TABLE OF CONTENTS

FOREWORD

Mark Harden, CFO, Eurasia and Africa Group, Head of Global Finance Transformation, The Coca-Cola Company (2011-17)

It has been over 20 years since I was first introduced to the ideas of large-scale systems transformation. In my career at The Coca-Cola Company, whether I was implementing systems, processes, and organizations; creating and leading new business models; or directing regional or global transformations, I needed strong methods, defined approaches, and robust tools that enabled us to make huge changes while bringing everyone along with us on each change journey.

I have worked with Paul and Garrick many times along the way and realized that mastery of change involved the melding together of art, science, discipline, and technology. I also came to realize that the approach they and their teams had put together had reached a level of breakthrough that was right for the time.

They work with large organizations, have powerful methodologies and utilize sophisticated and effective tools for enabling large sustainable transformations. Their formula includes well designed and executed design events that kick-start your strategy. These unique events are powerful ways to collaborate with senior leaders to align on strategy, plan the implementation of that strategy, and identify the most passionate people to lead the transformation. Following these events, their tools help motivate and engage the entire organization as you implement the change. These steps alone have proven to be a winning formula. But, by layering on their tools to enhance personal and organizational learning and self-improvement you get exponential and sustainable win-wins for your teams and company.

For the last ten years they have been developing digital tools for achieving the same outcomes online. These platforms and apps support the widely distributed, global, networked-based organizations of the future. They have bottled their original formula, updated it for the digital age and are sharing it with us in this book. Through design and testing in the real world they have established new principles and tools for leaders to:

- collaboratively make decisions and implement change without needing everyone in the same place, at the same time, all of the time;

- scale change at whatever level it is required, in an engaging way;

- enable continuous improvement and learning in global organizations.

In addition, they have built their model and tools in a way that puts control in the hands of the users, not consultants.

Their tools and approaches enable massive change on a global scale, shrink budgets and do so in a way that makes the most of the digital age. This is a book for everyone interested in understanding how to make large scale sustainable shifts happen.

Once again, they are ahead of their time… at the right time.

INTRODUCTION

The digital civilization

New technology has always propelled humans forward. Often, we are afraid of it. Take the invention of the steam train. When the Stockton to Darlington Railway, the first public steam railway, opened in 1825, people feared the worst: the human body wasn't designed to travel at the astonishing speed of 30 miles per hour and something dreadful would happen if it did. With the invention of the telephone, preachers in Sweden said the phone was an instrument of the devil, causing phone lines to be stolen or sabotaged; others feared that telephone lines were channels through which evil spirits would enter our homes.

In his 1960s classic book, *Understanding Media*, Marshall McLuhan accurately predicted the rise of mass media and the 'global village.' He described how 'electronic technology is reshaping and restructuring patterns of social interdependence and every aspect of our personal life'.

While McLuhan popularized this concept, he was not the first to think of it. Inventor Nicholas Tesla in an interview with *Colliers* magazine in 1926 stated:

> When wireless is perfectly applied the whole earth will be converted into a huge brain, which in fact it is, all things being particles of a real and rhythmic whole. We shall be able to communicate with one another instantly, irrespective of distance. Not only this, but through television and telephony we shall see and hear one another as perfectly as though we were face-to-face, despite intervening distances of thousands of miles; and the instruments through

1

which we shall be able to do this will be amazingly simple
compared with our present telephone. A man will be able
to carry one in his vest pocket.

Our civilization today is in the midst of a technology revolution that
is transforming every aspect of society. We have the potential to lead
richly connected lives. What type of society are we creating? Will
the rewards of digital go to an elite few, or will they be more evenly
distributed in a society in which everyone has the chance to play a
role and join the conversation? Will we create systems that alienate
the digitally disadvantaged? Will we enable everyone to participate in
society in a way they choose? Will we be able to live lives that best suit
our needs, our lifestyles and our working patterns?

As humans, we have a remarkable ability to absorb, use and become
accustomed to new technology. We also tend to take a benevolent view
of these technology inventions. When it's our car, washing machine,
hair dryer or central heating, we hardly recognize them as technology
at all. Would you prefer to get on a plane every time you want to
speak to your grandchildren in another country, rather than pick up a
telephone? Would you smash your spectacles as a gesture against the
rising tide of technology? Would you swap your central heating for a
fire in every room (which you have to make and tend each day)? In the
context of digital technology, why would you prefer to go to the library
a few miles down the road when you can access the biggest library in
history from the comfort of your own home?

Have we become a digital civilization? At what point will we have
too much technology?

Digital humans

In a recent interview, Bill Gates describes how in his view most of human
work will soon be conducted by automated technology. Our current
society based around jobs and work will fundamentally shift, he argues.
He asks, what will be our purpose as humans in such a world?

Many people are equally concerned about our future. The digital revolution we are currently experiencing is as profound as any revolution in history. Being a human on planet earth today is a different experience from what it was ten years ago. We can see the impact on politics, business and even personal relationships.

We believe we are entering the age of the digital human. As individuals, we live in a digital world rich in knowledge and data. We can access more worlds than any other generation could imagine. We can lead multiple lives with a degree of flexibility we have never enjoyed before. We can establish communities around all our different interests. We have more virtual friends than those we see day to day. Many of us are now free to work from anywhere. Technology already augments how we work and how we live. Soon it will be commonplace for technology to become integrated with our biological bodies (in some cases, it already is). Will we one day become more digital than human?

Digital organizations

What does digital mean for our organizations as we know them today? The fixed offices and bureaucratic institutions of the past decades in many ways already seem outdated. Will the glass skyscrapers that pepper our cities today become the empty cathedrals of tomorrow? Will we even need cities if no one needs to go into an office to work? In the meantime, what engages, motivates and gets the best from a human workforce, whilst it is knowingly acting as a stepping stone to the next wave of technology optimization?

The modern organization today is a global network of connections, knowledge, customers and suppliers. Ever changing and evolving, ever responding to new challenges and stimuli, we would describe organizations today as being, to all intents and purposes, 'alive.' There is barely such as thing as 'local' enterprise anymore: where digital is present, every organization, everywhere, is connected globally in some way.

In the past, organizational change or transformation was something done steadily, perhaps over several years. Organizations gradually moved into new markets or focused on becoming more competitive or productive. Change was 'done to' organizations by smart consultants with clever models and frameworks for strategic advice or process improvement.

Transformation itself is changing. Today, organizations need to move much faster. New threats appear without notice. Consumer sentiment changes overnight. New opportunities emerge and are quickly taken advantage of by fast-moving competitors. Organizations need to sense and respond to these changes without delay. They need to do so whilst not disrupting their core business or their people. It's this challenge that has seen hundreds of well-known brands disappear in recent years.

There is a sense of panic in some boardrooms. Messages can no longer just come from the top. Organizations are being de-bossed and hierarchies flattened. A new kind of leadership is required for digital humans that has more in common with how biological or nervous systems operate, rather than the mechanistic models of previous years.

We are already seeing the emergence of the chief digital officer (CDO). No longer relegated to just 'head of technology' or seen as a minor role on the board. The CDO now controls a vast domain that touches every part of the organization. When the day comes that an organization has more robots than people, will the chief human resources officer (CHRO) even be required? Will the post ultimately merge with that of the CDO to become 'head of digital and human resources'?

About us

It was December 2004. The world was emerging from the dot-com crash. Google had recently gone public, a new company called Facebook had just launched and we all still had Nokia mobile phones.

Since the mid 1990s we had been involved in the most sophisticated methods for enabling large scale system change through collaborative decision-making. It was (and still is) a set of technologies, processes, philosophies and principles used by governments, global organizations and NGOs to align, make decisions and scale. We recognized that the digital world was coming fast and the implications would be seismic. We asked ourselves the question, how do we achieve the same results virtually as those we can face-to-face. How do we enable thousands of people to work together and learn together when they are based in different locations around the world? At the same time, how can we design work so that it can fit with the way people want to work?

Our response was to design a new kind of consulting organization. One that could be entirely virtual, immediately global and have the scale to work alongside the biggest organizations in the world. We called our new company 'Ludic' from the Latin *ludo* meaning playfulness. If we were going to invent a new way of working, it should at least be fun.

In our work over the years, we have been asked questions such as:

- How do we engage our people across the globe?

- How do we, as leaders, make more informed decisions?

- How can we get the best from virtual global teams?

- How do we ensure strategic decisions are implemented?

- How do we work with diverse teams of young and old?

- How do we scale rapidly?

- How do we transform and innovate without disrupting?

- How do we shift from a centralized to a more decentralized system?

Often, we've been asked these questions because the usual answers have been tried by others before and proven unsatisfactory. We are researchers and inventors at heart. We love creating solutions. We see our organization as a lab and our response has often been to develop something new: a software platform, a method, a new environment.

We have had the privilege of working with many amazing people and clients who were prepared to try something different. Through these collaborations over the past decade, we have discovered how to activate organizations so that they can transform themselves – and what digital means in practice to the people who work with them.

Humans have achieved awe-inspiring things by working together. Digital enables us to collaborate like never before in history. It has radical implications for our global society. How have our societies in history succeeded or failed when faced with momentous changes? We are fascinated by these questions. That is why we've written this book.

About this book

This book is about the impact of digital on us as individuals and how we organize together to get things done. It is also about what we have learned about how to make the most of all that digital has to offer whilst avoiding its pitfalls.

The book consists of four parts, each of which addresses an important aspect of the digital organization. We start with understanding the context of our digital world. We then look at how individuals and organizations use digital to make and execute decisions across virtual teams; how to engage and motivate on a global scale; and finally how to provide the learning required to get us all to the next level.

The book is not intended to be an academic thesis nor a technical manual. Instead, it is a document of what we have learned, our experiences and the important principles we have synthesized over the past decade while working in this way. For example, you will find 12 principles that we believe form a blueprint to activate digital organizations.

We've tried to avoid jargon and to write a book that everyone might find interesting and accessible. At the end of the book, we've included our 'terms of art.' This provides our working definitions for the various technical terms that we use within the text. We've included links and sources where we think a reader might want to know more about a topic we've referred to.

It is, above all, a contribution to the conversation about our joint future, in the hope that we as humans will use the opportunities digital provides to create a future world we all want to live in together.

SECTION 1:

OUR FUTURE DIGITAL SELVES

1.

OUR BRAVE NEW DIGITAL WORLD

'O wonder!
How many goodly creatures are there here!
How beauteous mankind is! O brave new world,
That has such people in't'

William Shakespeare, *The Tempest*,
Act V, Scene I, ll. 203–206

Rise and fall of a civilization

It is the Spring equinox in the year 818 AD. At the appointed hour, the Mayan high priest at Chichen Itza slowly ascends one of the four staircases of the pyramid of Kukulkan, a giant temple named in honour of the feathered serpent deity. As the sun's shadow creates the illusion of the snake descending the pyramid, the priest gazes down upon the crowd of some 40,000 people. He begins a slow-hand clap. The crowd respond, the clapping builds to a crescendo. The echo from the top of the pyramid reflects the call of the resplendent quetzal, the sacred bird, across the city. A human sacrifice is made. The crowd is in rapture. The gods are pleased. It will be a good year.

A civilization way ahead of its time, the Mayans thrived for more than 3000 years. They were brilliant architects, mathematicians and astronomers. They invented the concept of zero. Their calendar was accurate to within one day every 6500 years. The Mayans had one of the most advanced writing systems of any ancient civilization. Their cities were centres for arts, science and religion, teeming with more than 2000 people per square mile (which is comparable to modern Los Angeles County). Their creation and adoption of highly sophisticated technology propelled them forward.

However, by around 900 AD the population had crashed. Perhaps as many as 95 percent of the Mayans had died and the great cities were deserted. Many theories exist as to the cause of this great decline. The leading hypothesis is that the Mayans simply over-extended themselves. They over-populated and over-farmed their natural resources, leading to deforestation and drought on a massive scale.

Like the Mayans, are we in danger of becoming the authors of our own demise? Will a future artificial intelligence record that 'for an unknown reason, at some point during the 21st century, biological humans seemed to stop building, producing or making – they scattered from their cities and by the mid 2100s had almost entirely ceased to exist.' Or will we have created a digital utopia that ensures our survival for the next millennia?

Our history is populated with stories like this. Technological change, upheavals and the promise of new worlds all harness our dreams of a better life. Professor Klaus Schwab, founder and executive chairman of the World Economic Forum, has suggested we are currently in the Fourth Industrial Revolution – the blurring of physical, technological and biological domains. The First Industrial Revolution transformed production with water and steam power. The Second brought electric power and mass production. The Third refers to automation and the shift from analogue to digital.

In the time of Elizabeth I and the discovery of what was called the new world, Francis Bacon published a story in which the positive and supportive relationships between people in Atlantis created a utopian society. It is little known that Shakespeare used this tract as a basis for the utopian portion of his play *The Tempest*. The genius of *The Tempest*, of course, is that his world is also populated with monsters.

When the Internet was first being built and http coding was all the rage, the dreams of a new society were projected onto it. It heralded a new age. We didn't imagine that the dark web might emerge or that the Internet could spawn just as many opportunities for criminals as prospects for entrepreneurs. In the shift to digital, we encounter both angels and demons.

The digital world has the capacity to unleash incredible human potential by connecting us to each other and to our vast array of knowledge. It promises open democracy and fairer access to resources for all. It enables massive parallel processing for problem-solving in society. It lowers barriers to entry for creating new innovations, new businesses and almost instantaneous launching of new services. These are the positive outcomes we strive for. The dangers to avoid, like the bleak future described in Aldous Huxley's *Brave New World*, include a future in which human life has been almost entirely industrialized. One in which society is controlled by a handful of people at the top of a world state. Where the Internet and debate is mediated by monopolistic and oligarchical forces. Where rights of access and the rights of freedom of information are skewed by self-serving policies that twist the neutral platform accessible to all into a monster that promotes only the interests of the few.

The shift to digital

The contours of our new world across business, society and nation states have been forever changed. Business today is an interconnected global ecosystem. A digitally connected human is likely to have as many 'friends' in places they've never been to as in their own town. Our supranational structures are shifting – Britain's relationship with Europe, the United States' and China's relationships with the world are in flux. Politicians are often seen to struggle with understanding this new reality as they rush to create policy that ensures safety, identity, security and growth. There is tension between our political institutions and businesses that are larger, wealthier and more powerful than many countries. We only have to look at the European response to Google and Microsoft in the courts, or the attempts to gather taxes from huge organizations that are able to shift financial structures to wherever it is most advantageous. Consider the backlash against Uber's ability to disrupt the protections that exist in the cab industry in a manner never anticipated by legislation.

At the time of writing, Apple's market cap is just north of $900bn, which would put it as the 17th largest national economy in the world, just ahead of the Netherlands, as measured by recent IMF data on global GDP. Amazon ($751bn) and Google ($745bn) would rank as the 18th and 19th largest economies respectively, ahead of international finance hub Switzerland, which has a $709bn valuation.

A brief digital history

It is a long way from 1965 when two computers at MIT Lab used packet-switching to communicate with one another for the first time. In 1973, global networking became a reality as University College London and Norway's Royal Radar Establishment connected to Arpanet. The term Internet was born. In 1974, Telenet become the first commercial Internet service provider (ISP). In 1987, the number of computers connected to the Internet exceeded 20,000. In 1990, Tim Berners-Lee, a CERN scientist developed Hypertext Mark-up Language (HTML), technology that continues to underpin how we navigate and use the Internet today. The following year, in 1991, CERN introduced the world wide web to the public. In 1995, Amazon, Craigslist and eBay went live and in 1998 the way we engage with the Internet changed entirely, with the launch of Google.

By the time the dot-com bubble burst in 2000, around 600 million users were online. In the aftermath, faster mobile data (3G) became commercially available and a new kind of online organization emerged, giving us social media as we now know it. Facebook launched in 2004, YouTube in 2005, Spotify in 2006 and more. Many of these original services have already been devoured (remember Friendster, MySpace, Diaspora and Del.icio.us?).

We see the current shift to what we now call 'digital' as starting in 2007 with the launch of a new kind of smartphone. Smartphones had been around since the late 1990s. NTT DoCoMo's smartphone had huge success in Japan. Nokia had also launched one. But with the launch of Apple's iPhone and HTC's device they began to scale massively. These phones had far better data capacities and large touch screens. Suddenly access to the Internet was mobile. A plethora of affordable devices quickly followed that meant entire populations could leapfrog decades of development to join the digital masses. In Africa, most people now own two or more smartphones. The cost of entry has continued to get cheaper.

In 2007 less than 10 percent of the world's population was on the Internet. In 2018 almost 50 percent of the world population was online and the number of smartphone users alone stood at 2.53bn, according to Statista.

In only half a century, we have changed the way we live, work, learn, connect, problem solve and communicate so dramatically that our world is unrecognizable from the time we first had personal computers. The extremity of this shift can be seen dramatically in places such as Rwanda and Uganda today. The optical-fibre backbone and wireless Internet was only turned on in 2010. Already, the younger generation's taste in dress, hobbies and music have more in common with their contemporaries in Brooklyn, New York, than their parents who are living an urban African or even tribal village lifestyle. As computer scientist Alan Kay said: 'Technology is anything invented after you were born'.

Impact on individuals

Digital has opened all of our eyes to a world of possibility. The access to knowledge, people, things and places means that we can bring dreams into reality that were never reachable or even conceivable before. New careers, opportunities, places to live and work are available. People can leapfrog social situations, they can use a smartphone to set up a global supply business and find out how to run it on YouTube for free.

Take, for example, the British millionaire estate agent Akshay Ruparelia, who set up an online estate agency while he was studying for his A levels. His company, Doorsteps, was privately valued at £12m in October 2017, after just one year of trading and is currently the 14th biggest estate agent in the UK.

Fraser Doherty set up SuperJam aged 14, selling homemade, organic, sugar-free jam to his neighbours. Based on his grandmother's jam recipe, Doherty has grown a brand that has become a global phenomenon, selling millions of pots and supplying thousands of supermarkets around the world.

There are millions of young people around the world who have caught the entrepreneurial bug. The ability to launch a business by simply creating a webpage and a supply network is revolutionizing the world and creating jobs for the next generation. It is spawning innovation and experimentation on a mass scale.

As we continue to transform our working world, what will we look to achieve as a society? How will we configure our organizations and institutions next?

Impact on organizations

People have organized themselves in many ways throughout history: tribes, armies, cities, nations, monarchies, democracies, clubs and societies. What happens when one type of organizational form meets another? What happens when armies meet guerrillas?

It was entirely appropriate for the European armies of the 18th century to fight in formation, given that they encountered each other in the open field and wore strikingly different uniforms to distinguish who was who in the heat of battle.

Yet, when the British fought the Native Americans in the wilderness of East Coast America, these tactics and rituals were inadequate. It's hard to imagine what the Native Americans – camouflaged, experts in stealth, fond of ambushing and entirely unpredictable – would have made of the brightly coloured targets who noisily marched shoulder to shoulder, line after line. Clearly, there are many dimensions to how we organize, but the most important principle is that our choice of organization must be appropriate for the context it inhabits. As context changes, so must we adapt.

In today's digital economy, old, rigid and inappropriate business models are being destroyed. Organizational models are emerging that take advantage of new tools and technologies as quickly as they are invented. The successful organizations of the future will be more like living systems. They will be able to adapt and respond to their markets and environments quickly and flexibly. They will be able to scale up and down as needed. It is one of the reasons we called this book *Alive*.

Digital has led the organizations of today to take many new and complex forms such as organic, freelance, knowledge-worker networks. They operate in a state of continuous flux that mutates to swarm around specific projects. This has been the norm in film-making and architectural work and is fast infiltrating every sector.

In the new digital world, organizations are beginning to have multiple forms within themselves, determined by what they are attempting to get done. They might adopt rigid top-down controls where that is required (for reasons of regulation or safety) while at the same time they may adopt matrix models that enable complex value chains to bring products to market. They might use flexible workforces, fixed teams, networks, open innovation, closed-loop development and more, depending on the outcomes desired.

The uniformity we used to expect from institutions is breaking down. We believe that organizations are becoming more tribal in their nature, gathering numerous different types of employment contracts within a single brand: full time, part time, agency or associates co-exist in one eco-system.

Workforces are also becoming more diverse. Age groups are more widely spread. Teams come from numerous countries. Personal situations such as single parenthood or caring for an older relative are more easily accommodated by the flexibility that digital working brings. In our research, we have found that many workers prefer to work from home or from bases outside a fixed office.

Employers find themselves managing a greater variety of relationships with all their different employees. If they are to attract and retain talent, they are having to learn to take a more personalized approach in how they engage their people. One size does not fit all in the digital world.

The identity and the culture of the organization has an impact on the talent that is attracted to its brand. At the heart of managing organizations today is the requirement to create an overarching narrative and identity that provides a sense of community and purpose. One of the most potent ways of doing this is through the set of tools, apps and platforms that combine to create the online, digital experience of work. The ability of this set of tools to connect people, provide access to knowledge, to account for the organization and to promote unique customer experiences is at the cutting edge of competitive behaviour between organizations in the digital world.

Digital challenges

For those who adapt to these digital challenges, the opportunities for finding new competitive forms are immense. Those organizations not making this shift risk a decline in performance or eventual extinction. The same is true for everyone working within organizations. What will be the new roles and how will we navigate in today's complex, interconnected world? How much will we be asked to work in different ways and employ new skills? Most importantly, how will organizations motivate, equip and engage their people and stakeholders in this brave new digital world?

History is littered with examples of organizations that could not adapt quickly enough or failed to see what was about to eat its lunch. Kodak did not fail because it missed the digital age. They actually invented the first digital camera in 1975. Unfortunately, Kodak took the view that they were primarily in the camera film business. They didn't realize that they were actually in the storytelling business. They held back for fear of hurting their lucrative film revenue and believed they could protect their massive market share with brand strength alone. By the time Kodak finally decided to commit to the digital game, it was too late.

It's alive

We find ourselves at a turning point in history. Our experience of being human has changed profoundly in the last ten years and is about to change as profoundly again in the next ten years. Our capabilities as humans are fast merging with digital. We already depend on our smartphones and wear digital devices to look after us. We will soon have digital companions to guide us through our work and lives.

In evolutionary terms, we are starting to think about how digital systems might literally, as well as figuratively, be coming alive and competing with us. When will artificial intelligence exceed our human capabilities? Commonly known as the 'singularity', Ray Kurzweil, a leading futurist and director of engineering at Google, expects it to occur by 2045. He expects a computer to pass the Turing test — the point at which a human cannot distinguish between whether we are interacting with a computer or a human — by 2029. At the point of the singularity, our digital world may not only be alive, it may be fully conscious.

Scary technological monsters

'If we want machines to think, we need to teach them to see.'

Fei-Fei Li

Many fear that humans will indeed be superseded by AI, robots and automation; that digital will disrupt our lives, destroy our jobs and our standards of living. These doomsday scenarios are entirely possible. Every major technological change in history has provoked violent responses and certainly disrupted old ways of working. So far though, each technological revolution has in the long run created new experiences and more jobs. Where people are given access to technology, it generally improves their lives.

Looking further ahead, Accenture, the management consultancy, estimated in early 2018 that if all organizations invested in AI and human-machine collaboration at the same rate as the top investing organizations, revenues could rise by 38 percent by 2022 and employment by 10 percent.

At a company level, the global director of manufacturing at Rolls-Royce, Hamid Mughal told Innovate UK in November 2017 that he saw three immediate benefits as digital systems start to think and decide for themselves: self-correcting systems, virtual design and service sensors.

Taken together, he thinks these improvements are likely to result in more employment: 'In the same way that earning a good living from designing computer games was unthinkable before it happened, we will see a re-deployment into jobs that we don't yet know.'

He sees humans continuing to play a significant role in all spheres of business in 50 or 60 years' time. 'Our intuitive thinking and softer skills will be even more important than today. When you are not constrained by location and can partner with whomever you want, how do you build long-term relationships? Trust will remain incredibly important to human beings no matter how automated we become in the future. Can robots in whichever form you take them resolve the long-term strategic value of the business? The application of strategy, knowledge and innovation is where people come in.'

Scary organizational monsters

The other form of monster for organizations is one of their own creation. Time and again, they launch new strategies, often costing millions of pounds, which fail to deliver against their objectives.

Organizations are experiencing, although in a milder form, the same fascination with the power of digital media as happened in the so-called Arab Spring in 2011. In post after post, picture after picture, the aspirations and grievances of a new generation came together to topple a series of autocratic regimes. Then, either in the form of hardliners or extremists, the regimes came back. Unfortunately for the protesters, no strategy was in place to harness all the commitment to the ideal of a more open society assembled through social media and on the streets.

Organizations often suffer from the same sense of energy-sapping let-down. They bring in every available form of social media, then rely on their employees to self-organize. This lack of structure in rolling out these tools, prevents their implementation against a set of strategic goals. Instead, results are usually random and unintended, undermining performance and disengaging followers.

A new model of consulting

Confronted by the challenge of digital transformation, the reflex of many organizations is to turn to the same consultants who have been advising them for the last 30 years. Their methodologies are still much the same as those pioneered in the 1990s. However, with the advent of real-time data, the days of strategy from the top, slideshow presentations and 2x2 matrices are passing swiftly. The consulting model itself is changing. Within the industry, the signs are everywhere. Profitability is under strain as pitches for contracts become a race to the bottom. The traditional model of large consulting teams working for months on end is outdated and is being replaced by new types of organizations with agile teams, powered by technology tools and platforms. Strange as it might seem, the consultants themselves might be sleepwalking into a crash, if they are not careful.

A new digital model is emerging that significantly disrupts and undermines the traditional consulting business. In our experience, successful transformation is no longer about externally led massive change programmes. For digitally enabled organizations, transformation is about building capability internally and lining up the right digital tools to enable the people to transform the organization themselves. For example, using a single software platform, organizations can provide a series of apps for virtual teams to unlock new knowledge, enable new processes and reinforce engagement. They can use virtual dashboards to provide feedback on results that are immediate and continuous. Strategy development is now happening in real time and the people who will be impacted the most are creating informed solutions themselves.

The advantage that consultants once had of accessing large numbers of specialists at relatively low cost is disappearing too. Organizations are less tolerant of standard solutions delivered by junior teams. They are also realizing that they can solve major transformational challenges by using digital platforms that only take two or three specialists to support. The process and content knowledge required is embedded in the technology. Instead of a programme team of hundreds, perhaps only five or ten are now required. We are not predicting the demise of consulting, just a radical change. What remains of the consulting team will be deeply experienced experts who bring their knowledge and access to the latest thinking. Consultants may also support the transformation by orchestrating, animating and nudging through digital platforms. In consulting, as everywhere else, job descriptions are being re-written. Digital is making some roles redundant, but also bringing new opportunities. We believe it is a case of adapt or die.

Conclusion

The history of work since the First Industrial Revolution is about humans being treated like machines in a system optimized for profitability and efficiency. Digital is a rising tide that is causing a sea change in how people are prepared to work. People want to be treated as individuals and with respect. They want to engage in work and live lives that give meaning.

We're entering a brave new digital world full of possibility but also of potential threats. In the chapters that follow we will address these fundamental questions.

- What do we value and what makes us thrive as humans?

- What enables organizations to deal rapidly with change, learn quickly and create new behaviours?

- If change is the new norm then how do we survive and gain competitive advantage by evolving with a purpose and direction, not turning into a self-organized monster?

So, we are more with Shakespeare and less with Huxley. We believe that we can summon up the powers to transform ourselves. As humans, we are not just originators of dazzling science but creatures of extraordinary imagination as well. Like Prospero, the challenge is for us to combine with digital technologies and conjure up new tools and new models to keep humans at the centre of the stage we have created for ourselves.

2.

LIVING IN A CHANGING WORLD

> In this chapter, we comment on 22 trends that we think are worth paying attention to. The impact of these trends echo throughout this book. We want to understand how they are disrupting our current lives and then explore the implications for how we might work, learn and live in the future.

Our assumptions about how our organizations and institutions operate are being re-written as we and they evolve in response to the changing digital reality. As Einstein said, the survivors will be those who adapt to new conditions. The best performers will seize the opportunity to leap far ahead. Those who are slower to adapt will find themselves challenged and possibly overwhelmed, by disruptive new types of organizations, unconstrained by any legacy systems.

We have organized these trends into three sections: next for tech, work and learning. We believe that the skills associated with learning are as fundamental to thriving in the digital realm as reading and writing were to survival in the post-agricultural era.

Next for tech

'All sorts of things can happen when you're open to new ideas and playing around with new things.'

Stephanie Kwolek

Trend 1: The merger of the physical and digital

The Internet is about to transform our lives again. As consumers, we already use it intensively. Now the Internet is being extended to the physical worlds of industry, infrastructure and cities.

Every device that we create is becoming connectable and every part in the chain of value is being connected. We have friends who own a kettle that communicates with the Internet. They can turn it on even while abroad. Connected lights, music systems and safety equipment are rapidly turning our homes into smart environments. In manufacturing, production is becoming more agile and automated. Maintenance will be pre-emptive – our machines are beginning to tell us what they need before we are aware of it. The upside is that all this connectivity will lead to greater energy efficiency. Everything is connected. The Internet of Things is a reality. We are already experiencing entertainment and shopping that is seamlessly personalized to our needs whenever we engage with movie streaming services. Those sci-fi movies where advertisements are tailored to the individuals walking past are not far off our everyday reality. Our cars already have settings that learn about our habits and desires and adjust accordingly. The new battery driven, possibly driverless, cars are not called electric – that was the past – they are now called electronic. They are more like an online mobile computer than a motor car. This reality is becoming commonplace across the globe. Siri, Alexa and all the other natural language gadgets that are moving into our lives are just the start of this phenomenon.

One of the consequences of this hyper-connectivity of people, technology and objects is the generation of data - masses of it. We are already beginning to see a global conversation about the use of this data. Referred to as the 'information age' or 'big data', the opportunities presented to the industry and manufacturing have long been anticipated and promoted. It is estimated that industry is only using 0.5 percent of currently available data. The consequences of more data use will be far-reaching. According to a recent report, *Made Smarter* produced for the UK government by the chief executive of Siemens UK, Jurgen Maier, the boost to British manufacturing could be £455bn accompanied by a cut of 4.5 percent in CO2 emissions.

As much as this reality is desired by big business, political realities are proving less pliant. The flow of data and the global connection of supply chains have political implications for countries. Where are data farms located? Who gets to tax the system? Which countries benefit from the work that may be generated? When systems are optimizing prices, affordability and efficiency, it becomes a winner-takes-all situation. This is often to the detriment of those unable to compete for reasons such as geography or lack of investment.

A more problematic consequence of the merger of the online and the physical is the application of big data principles, data harvesting and social media for social engineering and political purposes. The debate about the outcomes of the US election and the UK Brexit referendum possibly having been swayed by unregulated practices on social media is just getting underway. Policy, legislation and politicians are lagging behind the implementation of these technologies. At the moment we are living in an unregulated online wild west.

We assume that a fair democratic impulse is the purpose of all politics. We hope that the connection of the digital with the physical will have a democratizing impact on all societies as more and more people get used to the individual responsibility it brings. We believe that in time regulation will come, that a level playing field will be promoted for all of society and the unscrupulous will not thrive. The prize, according to Maier, is a new, vibrant and growing 'creation sector' which will form around digital technology, software, algorithms, digital media, games and agile factories.

Trend 2: Machines plus humans

Like the Internet itself, which was in use among universities in the early 80s, artificial intelligence has taken its time to reach the mainstream. It is now starting to make its impact felt. AI (otherwise known as cognitive computing or machine learning) opens up the capacity to make sense of all the unstructured data that is generated by our connected objects and systems.

We will be able to do much more of what we were doing already. Predictive analysis, for instance, is now significantly more powerful and accessible. It is having a powerful impact in the medical industry and saving lives.

Here's an irony though: costs don't necessarily fall. The use of AI in cameras on every phone might be popular, but improved functionality requires additional data processing, which in turn demands more power. The energy required to process digital picture-making is significantly more than what was required to process old fashioned film in chemical laboratories.

Some might fear the threat of AI to us as humans, but it is not machine consciousness – yet. Rather, at this stage it amplifies human intelligence and permits us to operate at a different scale. Genome sequencing, for example, is now computerized and performed with optimized sequences for reading the information in a fraction of the time it once took.

'We have to reap the benefits while avoiding the pitfalls,' says Stuart Russell at the Centre for Human Compatible AI. 'As soon as you put things in the real world with self-driving cars or digital assistants … as soon as they buy things on your behalf or turn down appointments, then they have to align with human values.' Values-based coding of AI or friendly AI is a growing and significant trend amongst the coding community. However, not everyone can be relied on to code in the best interests of humanity.

Elon Musk in a recent documentary warns that we could have an AI hedge fund that could maximize its value by shorting consumer stocks, going long on defense manufacturers and starting a war.

It is clear that optimized AI systems will need to have values even if humans are not always the best role models. Our values vary: some of us eat meat, some of us don't. Ethics courses are becoming a key component of coding education.

Using AI, we are starting to develop smarter solutions to major challenges such as food shortages, waste, health and wellbeing. Data is becoming more transparent. Goods and services are becoming more personalized and easier to use. Our creativity, such as making music or visualizing ideas, is being enhanced.

We are already seeing the explosion in creativity that has emerged in video-making with the advent of YouTube and Vimeo, the music-making that comes from access to software such as Propellerhead's Reason, or the composition tools such as Sibelius. We believe that the future of humanity is an explosion of our creativity facilitated by AI and other tools.

So the future will most likely be determined by the way we choose to combine the capabilities of machines and humans. What about those who wish to use it against the good of all? We are pragmatists. We believe that the transparency promoted by the mass of feedback and data presented by the web will, over time, lead to fairer systems for all.

Trend 3: The rise of the robots

Robotics lies at the heart of the transformation of industry and society. By 2019, it is expected to be an industry worth $135bn a year and growing by 17 percent per annum. Much of the action is in Asia, where Japan and China are re-tuning their entire manufacturing sectors by replacing workers in their factories with robots. In Germany, the broader ElecTech sector, defined as hardware combined with electronics and software, accounts for 35 percent of all innovation.

Industrial robots have been with us in making cars for some time. As computing power increases and smaller designs can be engineered, co-bots (collaborative robots) that are nimble enough to move around and among us are emerging in hospitals and in services.

We will find ourselves interacting with three types of robot:

- ones that work with us or in place of us, such as those in manufacturing;

- ones we use as remote humans taking us to hazardous or extreme environments; and

- those that act like a prosthesis that augments us and make us stronger.

It is the equivalent of the shift we experienced from the mainframe to the PC, and from the PC to the handheld smartphone. Advances in visioning software and machine learning are letting robots live beyond the constraints of the manufacturing world. At time of writing, more than 20 percent of US homes have voice-activated assistants in the form of Amazon's Alexa or Apple's Siri. Robots don't have to look like humans either. Just look at the rise of the drone and the applications being found for them in everyday life, whether in the media, for leisure, entertainment or in transporting objects.

As we have noted already, work as we know it is undoubtedly being changed by the mass use of robots, putting numerous jobs at risk in knowledge and in industry. In a 2013 study, Carl Benedikt Frey and Michael Osborne examined the vulnerability of 702 occupations. They found that 47 percent of jobs in the US were at risk; 35 percent in the UK (which is more oriented towards creative fields) and 49 percent in Japan. A plethora of recent studies into the impact of automation has been conducted with similar findings.

The impact on our workforce is that we are likely to see a significant split in job prospects between those with high and low levels of digital skills. Lack of digital accessibility is one issue leading to digital illiteracy. People without access are in very real danger of becoming a hugely disadvantaged under class. The fight for access to technology, information and resources, together with the perception of changes afoot is leading to unrest, mass migration of people and shifts to conservative or reactionary politics.

Before we get too gloomy, history indicates that automation in previous industrial revolutions has led to the creation of more jobs, not less, as resources are released for other tasks. Think of ATMs, for instance. As the costs of banking fell, more branches were opened all over the world. In the Industrial Revolution, automation led to the creation of many more jobs beyond agriculture. The development of adding machines led to the development of modern banking and insurance industries. These days there are many more people working from home who are trading commodities, stocks and shares, futures and options, than were ever able to fit on the trading floors of New York, Shanghai or London. In 2015, the World Bank estimated that the UK would need 745,000 workers with digital skills. According to Tech City UK, the digital sectors are creating jobs 2.8 times faster than the rest of the economy with starting salaries 36 percent above average.

Automation tends to re-define jobs, rather than destroy them. The need for re-education and skills building is a huge growth market and will help individuals and society adjust accordingly.

Trend 4: Algorithms

Algorithms are now assuming a pivotal, and often mysterious, role in our lives. Mathematical in origin, they are not as specific as formulas. They are more like a set of rules or recipes. Unlike a programme, which specifies each step, algorithms can be applied more generally to wider sets of data, performing calculations, processing data and automating logic.

Algorithms can be used to make predictions, which are then tested against other data to refine the findings. In machine learning, data is filtered through a series of layers, each layer improving the accuracy of the predictions.

Algorithms encode the physical world in the way that coding creates software for computers. They regulate the logistics of buses or trains in the transportation network. Mimicking natural models, such as the optimization of routes to food created by ants, logistical algorithms are able to direct concrete mixers through traffic in cities to guarantee delivery within five-minute windows.

Some algorithms are like the rock-stars of the applied mathematics universe. John von Neumann cracked sorting of data in 1945 when he created the Merge Sort algorithm that uses divide and conquer to solve problems arising from massive data sets. Fourier algorithms transform signals from time-based data to frequencies, a function that is behind absolutely everything we do in the digital realm. *Dijkstras* algorithm helps us find the fastest way between two points in a complex system. The security of the Internet is enabled through the cryptography of the ubiquitous RSA algorithm. It protects our banking data and is working each time we see a URL starting https. In the future, algorithms based on quantum computing will provide even greater security. Link analysis algorithms enable our Netflix account to present us with options that we are more likely to choose and enable Google to rank pages just for us. All feedback-based automation systems are defined by the Proportional Integral Derivative algorithm. It ensures systems like the control loop feedback mechanisms that keep airplanes stable in flight. It is behind most other systems that automatically modulate themselves against their goals, such as ABS breaking and safety mechanisms that we experience daily.

Algorithms are not free from criticism. Some feel that too much weight is given to samples that are too small. Others argue that they create prophecies that fulfil themselves. More alarming, the Harvard mathematician Cathy O'Neill revealed in her book, *Weapons of Math Destruction*, how algorithms were manipulated on Wall Street in the run-up to the 2007 financial crash in the interests of financial insiders.

Nevertheless, algorithms already define our everyday experience of the digital world. Nestlé encoded the coffee making algorithm into a capsule in its Nespresso system and prompted a coffee-making revolution. Algorithms will become simpler, more sophisticated and ubiquitous.

Trend 5: Modularization

Everything is becoming a pop-up. Restaurants, galleries, rock concerts, festivals, conferences are all here today, gone tomorrow. We have created sophisticated, highly configurable, plug-n-play infrastructure that can be deployed rapidly as and when required. Apps, components and processes are plugged on a project by project, task by task, basis. Modularization in the form of flat packs has transformed the market for home furnishings. Now it is being widely applied in education, architecture and engineering. The world is becoming a vast Lego set that can be assembled at speed and scaled up when required.

Modularization in industry, in the form of the 3D printing of individual parts (or additive manufacturing), is an integral part of the fourth industrial revolution. As Made Smarter reported, 3D printing is radically transforming certain manufacturing lifecycles, opening up the potential for rapid prototyping, radical design innovation, more efficient tooling, reduced time to market and lower production costs.

We believe it will be the modularization of manufacturing that will have one of the greatest impacts on our current society. Micro-production units, facilitated by robots and rapid manufacturing methods will begin to pop up on street corners. Perhaps the high street will be transformed from places of consumption to places of production. They are currently in peril as more and more goods are purchased online for direct delivery. This is a logical solution to the death of the traditional High Street.

In the future, we will probably define our individuality through our personal algorithms. We will choose recipes for products online and have them manufactured at a micro unit somewhere near us. We imagine that before long, everything from small cars to shoes, from clothing to communication devices, will be produced in this way. Vast arrays of modular, pop-up, micro-production units will spring up all around us, as ubiquitous as the local café.

Trend 6: Hyperlocal

We now have the potential to live highly individualized lives supported by a global infrastructure. All of the services with which we surround ourselves can be tailored to our own preferences without putting any restrictions on the extent to which we participate in the workplace or pursue any other interests.

We can choose to live within numerous different tribes, becoming members of multiple communities and even assuming different identities. Our technology supports all of these activities. Our products can be designed to our particular requirements. Our medicines are being personalized for each of our metabolisms and genetic profiles. Our food can be grown locally.

Design may take place all over the world, but before long, almost everything will be able to be manufactured very close to where we live and work. That which cannot be manufactured locally will be delivered in hours.

An example of hyperlocal is the concept of continuous productive urban landscapes (CPULS). First described by the architects Bohn & Viljoen in 2004, CPULS are an urban design concept that utilizes open space and disused sites to integrate local food growing into city planning.

Whether or not political globalization continues, organizations will compete on how well they are able to meet our growing desire for experiences, products and services customized on demand.

Trend 7: Neuroscience and behavior economics

Neuroscience is creating a radical set of insights into how we learn and how we behave, all of which are having profound implications on how organizations set about achieving their goals.

It is only in the last 20 years that the brain has taken a more central role in the science of learning. Through research into how the brain develops, we now know that:

- Our brains can remain 'plastic' as we age and adapt as we learn new skills, so we can continue learning however old we are and there is less need to start as early as possible.

- Our brains are as adept at learning indirectly as directly, extracting information from the environment that surrounds us.

- We innately search for meaning by creating patterns in which emotions play a strong role.

- The brain's creation of meaning depends on regular processing of these rich experiences.

- The brain thrives when immersed within rich experiences.

- The brain learns best in a state of 'relaxed alertness', during which time it responds well to challenges and poorly to threats.

- Games and simulations support 'fluid intelligence' in solving problems and improving memory. For example, in tests, surgeons who played video games were found to make 37 percent fewer errors.

These insights are opening up questions about education, learning and training. Dramatic progress is being made in understanding our behaviours. One implication has seen the adoption of nudges and pivots as tools for managing complex systems.

As Richard H Thaler and Cass R Sunstein argued in their 2008 book, *Nudge: improving decisions about health, wealth, and happiness*, we respond better to indirect encouragement and enablement, rather than direct instruction or enforcement. So subtle changes in the communication of strategy can lead to more of us adopting a whole series of desired behaviours more willingly. The reason why this is an important trend is because change will have to take place within massively connected and complex networks or systems. Self-organization of these systems may not necessarily lead to outcomes that are optimal or desirable for humans or society. Our increased understanding of neuroscience and behaviours will enable the subtle shifts required to enable massive changes within these systems.

Next for work

Trend 8: Digital media

The next generation's primary point of reference is more likely to be YouTube than Wikipedia. They prefer videos with step-by-step demonstrations of how something is done in practice, rather than to read about the theory. Older people soon get the idea, with a little confidence building from someone or something to guide them. The future of work will inevitably involve digital media to share knowledge and information.

Digital media is now in the hands of everyone. As a process, communication at work is becoming two way, not just top down. The implications for leadership are profound. Old models of power are being completely redefined. We cannot think of any examples where the sharing of knowledge and access to expertise and peer groups will not be augmented by digital media. We had considered that pottery might be an exception, before we discovered that advances in virtual reality (VR) and haptics has led to a VR experience in which it is possible to mould and create digital creations as if working with real clay. The experience is said to be every bit as satisfying as getting one's hands around wet clay if you like that sort of thing. The objects are then printed. Advances in 3-D printing mean that even clay can be printed as objects and then fired.

Trend 9: Play spaces

Our physical spaces for work will not disappear. They are being transformed. They are becoming flexible and knowledge-rich, allowing multi-disciplinary teams to work together more easily. Particularly when supporting innovation or learning, they are becoming closer to a production studio and a creative laboratory. Our social spaces are transforming too. Informal club spaces are not just for entertainment and leisure but are also becoming work spaces. More and more people are choosing to work from home as they can be as connected there as in the office. However, the need to get together is not going away. When we do get together, our social needs are more playful, encouraging collaboration and creativity. For example, an insurance agent may work from home, but the development of new insurance products requires collaboration. Implementation requires training and learning. All of which requires spaces for learning and play.

Formal work spaces are changing too. Frank Duffy the English architect famously predicted this development by defining the new work space as requiring spaces for collaboration, hive working, playing together, club spaces for informal work, cells for individual work and so on.

The Speed Factory developed by Adidas, the sportswear brand, is a prime example. All the disciplines in sports gear and health are brought together within a new type of open space in which knowledge can openly, instantly and richly evolve. New products are prototyped and tested by expert users. Data is generated and fed back into the design process on huge data screens, featuring real-time information graphics that facilitate the design process.

Trend 10: Community lives

The working spaces of the 20th century are also changing. We no longer need people to be cogs in a machine. Pioneered by architects like Frank Lloyd Wright and corporations like IBM, organizations were designed as large physical computing systems in which people came together to process large amounts of data. Computers now do the heavy lifting. Many more people are free to be mobile and to organize their work around their lives like never before.

We are now free from the limitations of physical space. In the 21st century, the place where we work is becoming more like a village. All the elements within our everyday lives can be brought together, such as where to look after the children and where to socialize.

As well as supporting our personal lives, our work can now locate itself wherever we happen to be. We no longer have to work continuously to process and organize data from a desk.

Rather than being linear, work is more fuzzy, lumpy and parallel. Within modern working spaces, we are free to do more and can work on different challenges simultaneously. Neither do we have to feel that we are losing our minds, alienated, or ignoring our families. How much more pleasant it is to work in an environment where our community is around us?

Trend 11: Global design

As systems and apps take on more process-based work, we are free to get more involved in design and development at a global level. One design team could be in London; the other in Tokyo. They share a skill base and a design language, all working from the same global database.

A team in Frankfurt, Los Angeles and Bangalore can work around the clock to design new equipment. They design changes, react to tests, create new solutions, update drawings, run simulations and print 3D models – in a continuous 24-hour cycle.

This is becoming the norm rather than the exception. The advent of local micro-production will enable countries that have fallen behind in manufacturing to leapfrog the current investment in factory automation, to compete once again on the global stage.

Trend 12: Local fabrication

Production is shifting to where the user is. The ability to incorporate local manufacture changes the approach to supply, especially for micro-batching and highly personalized products. Instructions for the manufacture of a product can now be sent anywhere in the world, to be manufactured locally, often in highly individualized batches, thanks to 3D printing.

Running shoes are already being produced by local manufacturers on street corners, instead of in a single large factory in China. They are printed and knitted on the basis of manufacturing recipe cards that are available around the world. Customers choose their products online and select where and when they want them produced.

The same is happening in health care, as medicine becomes more personalized. Molecules can be synthesized for specific metabolisms and produced in micro-labs associated with a local medical practice.

Contact lenses can be manufactured instantly at the local optometrist, clothes fabricated at a local clothing shop. Locally-grown fresh produce will shift farming away from massive hydroponic fields under plastic.

Trend 13: Swarming

One person solving one problem one step at a time might have been an approach that worked yesterday. Now we are relying on mass parallel processing, because it is proven to yield better outcomes and more robust solutions. Clouds of agents who attack a problem are much more likely to ensure it is solved faster and better.

These models of problem solving come in various guises, such as crowdsourcing, collaborative working or iteration. They follow the principle that we fail better when we fail faster.

From computer programming, as well as neuroscience, experience has shown that a more effective problem-solving approach is to swarm round a challenge to develop multiple, low-fi solutions which can be tested quickly. Then to move rapidly towards sharing knowledge and an understanding of what will work in reality.

For this model to be successful, organizations will depend on creating ecosystems of physical and virtual environments which are rich in knowledge and which are comfortable with higher degrees of ambiguity than organizations might once have tolerated.

Trend 14: Companion tools

In our digital lives and careers, we won't be alone. Companions of one type or another will be on hand to assist us in getting work done. They are already replacing the role of the manager. There are certainly ethical and practical questions regarding the level of transparency of data these tools provide about their human companions.

Our companions will not be just physical robots. Companion tools will give us the knowledge support where we need it in the form that we need it. iPads, dashboards and apps are already providing unstructured access to rich information.

Together, these different forms of companion (robots, dashboards and apps) will augment the reality we experience as humans. You may have seen the images of the Apollo astronauts working from the process books on their sleeves. Digital companions are dynamic, media-based versions of these famous manuals.

Trend 15: Lifelong learning

Because rapid change is now such a constant, lifelong learning is becoming a norm for everyone. As a 2017 report on trends in learning from the Open University noted: 'Employees and organizations cannot afford to keep still – the modern workplace needs agile, adaptable employees.'

Many organizations have found themselves spending heavily on developing elearning solutions that fail to meet their objectives for teaching strategically relevant skills. Perhaps elearning can excel at narrow technical challenges but for anything more qualitative, it is proving too one dimensional and fails to engage employees.

New blended solutions are being developed that make learning more immersive, on demand and flexible. The abilities to learn and to apply knowledge quickly will be core skills of digital literacy.

Trend 16: Universal basic income

More broadly and controversially, a universal basic income has long been on the agenda, raised by social philosophers as diverse as Thomas More, John Stuart Mill and Milton Friedman, as well as more recently by Joseph Stiglitz and controversially derided by Thomas Piketty.

At a time of massive technological change and social dislocation, the theory is that a universal basic income would give everyone a safety net, allowing people to adapt and re-train. When universally available, such a scheme would become easier to administer and less susceptible to fraud. Trials have already been conducted in Finland, Hungary, Scotland, Canada and elsewhere.

Socially, it would have significant benefits. With the comfort of a basic income, citizens would be freed up to contribute their time to their communities more than they would otherwise be able to, thereby strengthening social relations and reducing the costs of care. Some children would have a better start in life as well.

Economically, it could make increasing sense. If AI and robots are performing many of the tasks for which humans were once paid, who will be left to consume the goods and the services on which economies depend? As Aldous Huxley described in Brave New World, consumption is good: one of the key rationales for life is to increase consumption, to keep the economy growing.

For many universal basic income represents an elegant response to the continuing growth of inequalities and the rise of the digitally disadvantaged. We know from our history that a clash between the haves and the have-nots is fraught with danger.

Next for learning

As digital humans, we are making a transition not unlike the shifts made by our ancestors from hunter gatherers to farmers and then from farmers to factory workers. Those who thrive as individuals and as organizations will be those who can develop the right set of competencies that thrive in the new digital reality.

For learning professionals, the challenge is how they can best design programmes that satisfy these digital challenges and enable everyone to acquire the relevant skills at scale and at speed.

Trend 17: Experiential learning

As adults, we learn best when we are doing, actively solving problems or making models, rather than just assimilating content. Direct experience relevant to the context in which we lead our professional lives gives a practical understanding of the skills or the knowledge we are acquiring, which we can then supplement with the underlying theory.

Technologies such as virtual reality and augmented reality are adding new dimensions to the experience and reality of learning.

Trend 18: Gamification

The next generation is heavily exposed to gaming and is comfortable with virtual reality. Both are now integral to how we design learning programmes, platforms and experiences. Teaching through lectures looks to have a limited future. Games have been shown to have very high levels of learning retention. The reinforcement of learning in a game-based situation is well proven. Gamifying any learning situation increases the fun factor, the engagement and allows us to practice in a safe space.

Trend 19: On-demand learning

At the counter in a coffee shop, baristas watch instructional films describing how to create fancy patterns on top of coffee. In the same way, through their mobiles, they can access training apps, management information, accounting software and links to friends who can help them. For any kind of situation from strategy to production, we will be able to access an app to help in every aspect of our work. This experience will only become more available for everyone from accountants to zoo-keepers.

Trend 20: Apps and heuristics

Organizations are producing their own set of tools that are contextually relevant to their workplace. This is where learning support is now heading. Such platforms require focus. Organizations cannot expect their people to start using them or to self-organize. Under pressure in the workplace, the workforce will access the tools only if they need them or link them into a social group. Otherwise it's just introducing an additional layer of complexity that helps no one. Heuristics are like algorithms for humans. They create rules of thumb and sequences for people. Not so much as task sets and workflows, but most efficiently as aide-memoires that work like a language of models that enable individuals to function even when the environment is shifting about them continuously.

Trend 21: New environments for learning

Understanding new behaviours required for new situations is best achieved through simulation and play. We are creating learning environments, both physically and online, that allow for simulations in the form of scenarios, re-ordering information, testing alternative worlds, forming hypotheses and playing games. In whatever form, simulation spaces will be bringing together the resources and materials required for models, projections, break-outs and role plays. Our physical environments are going to facilitate play, recreation and collaborative learning. The more we collaborate online, when we physically come together, it will be for much more specific purposes.

Trend 22: Personalized blended learning

In learning, people respond best to rich contexts that allow for the creation of small believable worlds in real time. Technology already allows for the design of learning experiences tailored around each individual. At speed and at scale, we can now sequence dynamic combinations of games, animations, events, activities and challenges, all supported by feedback and coaching.

Through personalized blended learning, we can digitally reach large cohorts at a fraction of the price of face-to-face interaction without losing a sense of personal immediacy and connection. In preparing for the world of tomorrow, personalized blended learning is leading to better results, better experiences, more connected communities and more engagement.

Conclusion

Everywhere we look around us, the old ways are transforming and a new world is emerging. We have the tools to equip ourselves to make a smooth transition to this new digital reality. Those organizations that are now exploring how best to respond will be those who are going to be ready for all the challenges that lie ahead. It is not just the transformation of work, it is also the transformation of our societies and how we will equip ourselves to learn. The language and skills associated with learning will have a major impact on which societies will make the most out of the opportunities available in the digital world.

3.

THE ACTIVATED ORGANIZATION

'It's so weird to be alive and to be inside a body.'
Alejandro Jodorowsky

This chapter introduces the principles we propose for organizations to transform themselves. We ask what are digitally activated organizations able to achieve that old style organizations could not and how should organizations prepare themselves to make the leap?

Digital winners

The brave new digital world is, without doubt, creating winners and losers. As with any evolutionary jump, those individuals and tribes who can't or won't evolve and adapt will be left behind.

Naturally, we are all asking questions about our future prospects as our work and our lives are digitally transformed. The same applies to our organizations. Can they continue to exist in their present form? How inevitable is their future disruption? How can they learn to shed legacy systems and re-invent themselves without jettisoning their core sense of purpose?

At present many strategies for digital transformation under-deliver. Shifting to digital is not business as usual with a new tagline. Digital transformation requires a significant shift in the mindsets of leadership. Flying a plane is very different to managing a swarm of drones. Those who are surviving and prospering in the digital world are now following a different, more adaptive set of rules. They operate like entrepreneurs and designers who are instinctively comfortable within complex systems. They live within networks of value that can absorb, test and expand ideas as they happen. They enjoy experimentation. They are free from a pre-determined set of boundaries and expectations. They are focused like never before on both the customer outcomes and the employee experience across the entire organization.

Of ants and termites

The Soul of the White Ant was written in 1905 by South African Eugene Marais. Based on years of study into the behaviour of termites, Marais discovered that the way these seemingly simple creatures live and work together displayed qualities similar to those of a highly complex single organism. A termite nest is a complete world of defined hierarchies, roles and rules, within which the termites operate. The queen's role is that of the brain, the rest of the termites have other unique roles, which can be thought of as the mouth, teeth, claws, digestive system and blood cells of a larger organism. It is as if the cells of the body are independently mobile. Marais observed that these nest structures are created not through a top-down instruction but emerge from the day-to-day activities of their inhabitant insects.

Nearly a hundred years later, in his book *Out of Control* (1994), Kevin Kelly applies similar ideas to how organizations, computers and other systems had become more organic in their structures. He describes these organizations as complex adaptive systems: ones that respond to the environment or context in which they exist.

The human brain is a complex adaptive system that enables us to process billions of data points at any given time without causing us to short-circuit. Why, for instance, amongst the thousands of conversations we might overhear in parallel, when we hear our own name, do we immediately focus on that word? At our brain stem, we have a bundle of nerves referred to as the 'reticular activating system' (RAS). Its job is to filter out any unnecessary information,

42

prioritizing the important, relevant information we need at any given moment.

We are now in the midst of a digital revolution. Digital organizations are now more than just organic in structure, as we mentioned earlier, they are in fact, to all intents and purposes alive. Chris Meyer and Stan Davis proposed that this would happen in their 2003 book It's Alive: The Coming Convergence of Information, Biology and Business. We believe this has now become reality. Digital organizations have become a synthesis of human and digital. They have intelligence, artificial and human. Their workers are human and automated robots. Processing is done by humans and software. We can recognize many such systems at work in our day-to-day lives: think about how our cities, banks, transport, schools, shops and economies work.

Old and new together

During a recent visit to Tokyo, we experienced this high-tech, fast-paced, intensely modern city as a fantastic example of a system where humans and technology live and work together symbiotically. In Tokyo, digital adds to the experience of life rather than replacing it, whilst maintaining the cultural traditions that define the Japanese identity.

There is not much about Tokyo that is not automated or doesn't run like clockwork. As a foreigner, it is possible to navigate Tokyo almost entirely with the tools available on a smartphone. The city provides apps with current events and dynamic transportation information, even where parking spots are available. There are apps for translation that allow for easy – sometimes hilarious – communication. Using Google maps as a platform we were able to traverse the railways, buses and metro systems. A simple query into Google maps yields an answer that includes time, platform, directions and specific cost of tickets in yen. Without such an organizing set of apps, Tokyo is almost incomprehensible to the foreigner.

There are 38 million people who live in Tokyo, the largest conglomeration living together on the planet. Yet, because of the Japanese sense of personal space and mutual respect, we seldom felt crowded, even within large crowds. We went to the Meiji Shrine at New Year, without realizing we would share the experience with over one million people that day. Not once did we feel crowded or jostled, and everyone had an opportunity to pay their respects.

The Japanese have a highly collaborative culture. Sometimes, they are criticized for too much homogeneity, but we think there are many elements of their culture that are making them winners in the digital economy.

Japan has a concept called 'living national treasures.' These are people who have mastered a particular craft or cultural discipline to such an extent that their knowledge is regarded as of national importance. There are living national treasures for the performing arts such as Noh drama, kabuki theatre, music and dance. The craft skills cover ancient techniques such as sword making, pottery, lacquer work, kimono dyeing and paper making. Young people are connected to these experts in society via apprenticeships to ensure skills are transmitted to future generations, young and old working together. They have a fantastic and pragmatic understanding of multi-generational working.

The Japanese are very much a work-hard, play-hard society. There is something that the Japanese understand about games. It is no surprise that the world's first widely successful computer games and game companies originated in Japan. Playing games is woven into the culture. Launched in 1978, Space Invaders was instrumental in turning a novelty niche into a global industry. Pacman followed in 1980. Today, two of the three leading players in the category, Sony and Nintendo, are Japanese.

The Japanese also invented the concept of kaizen or continuous improvement. It is a concept of life-long learning. There is always something new to discover and the process of learning is continually valuable throughout our lives. The Japanese are renowned for their commitment to making things as perfect as they can be. Even when something is broken, they have the centuries-old craft of *kintsugi* which is the art of repairing broken pottery with gold, making the broken thing more beautiful when repaired than it was before.

The Japanese understand the power of small things, where 'everything speaks.' Take the Japanese tea ceremony for example. Every participant has a high degree of personal responsibility in ensuring that everything is completed properly. To prepare the tea requires diligent following of a set of pre-defined movements. The tea ceremony is not about drinking tea, but about the preparation of the tea with utmost care, designing the entire experience around the guests. Perhaps the Japanese tea ceremony has been one of the influencers of our digital world. The tea ceremony grew out of Zen Buddhism, which had, as is well known, a profound influence on Steve Jobs. We wonder if Steve Jobs' commitment to and implementation of, the rigorous simplicity of Zen and quality in every part of the experience has helped us make the shift from computers, which were for programmers, to digital, which is an experience for all, designed explicitly around the user.

Even though the future comes quickly, the Japanese embrace digital technologies whilst successfully preserving the best things about their cultural history. They apply what they know from the past to take advantage of the opportunities presented by the future.

We have learned two lessons from our experiences in Japan. Firstly, the Japanese embrace digital technologies, and when they do so, they don't lose their culture, their soul or their freedoms. Secondly, they aren't afraid of new technologies. When the Japanese began installing the Shinkansen or bullet train network in the 1970s, they were ahead of everyone. The high-speed train network not only provided fast links to the main cities, but its existence helped usher in many other innovations and technologies throughout the country. When it comes to new technology, like the first steam railways, we are often afraid and usually we don't need to be. We only need to turn it into what we want it to be. Though digital technology is heralding a brave new world, it is backed by thousands of years of human experience in the pursuit of cultural aspiration.

Complex evolving systems

There is a lot to be learned from how other large networked structures adapt and evolve. These structures can often be characterized by principles found throughout nature, across chemistry, biology, physics and mathematics and are often referred to as complex evolving systems.

A coral reef is one example of a complex evolving system. Left to its own devices, it will successfully self-manage with each coral, every fish and plant playing a specific role. Reefs change continuously. For example, the behaviours of the various elements of a reef even adapt to changing conditions, such as shifting to a different food source whilst its primary food recovers.

A complex evolving system is one that given a new stimulus (a change in priorities, a new goal) will automatically re-organize itself to achieve that new state until given another stimulus. These systems have the following dominant qualities:

- They have sufficient variation (i.e. not too homogenous).

- They can self-organize using simple rules.

- They have sufficient connectivity without becoming overly rigid.

- They can co-evolve alongside other as competing and complementary systems.

- They change over time by trial and error with new results emerging rather than being defined from the outset.

Another example of a complex evolving system is a jazz band. Multiple talents and virtuosos can play together if they are all working within a consistent musical framework and musical language. They can keep the overall group harmonized and bring in the right themes at the right time. They are constantly receiving feedback from each other and the audience, so they can self-regulate their tempo, volume and timing. A good jazz musician can join any jazz band anywhere. This is because jazz has a complex theoretical language that is itself based on a very simple set of rules. (For those interested in the theory, these rules were documented in a book in 1953 called the *Lydian Chromatic Concept of Tonal Organization* by George Russell). The system was established with Miles Davis, Ornette Coleman, Dizzy Gillespie and other greats who were playing and performing in New York at the time. An understanding of this musical language, alongside a book of jazz standards, is all it takes to create music in this way.

We think that there are direct lessons to be learned from jazz, as we begin to learn how to make the most of the digital tools we have created. Laptops and apps are the equivalent of musical instruments. Collaboration platforms are the equivalent of the stage. Collaborating processes, decision-making algorithms and creative processes equate to sheet music for specific songs.

When a group of people and technologies become well connected with sufficient knowledge, a common language and a shared purpose, the conditions are ripe for the system to change state. The complex evolving system is more agile, able to take advantage of emergent ideas and to scale rapidly.

The good news is that an organization can easily adopt the principles of complex evolving systems and use these as the catalyst for change. In this way, even very large organizations can orchestrate multitudes of experts and tools existing in multiple places.

Harnessing complexity

In today's digital world, the opportunities for harnessing complexity are greater than ever before. Meanwhile, challenges are ever present and can easily come with high cost or even failure.

Organizations of any size, from the local shop to a multinational business can tap into an ecosystem of suppliers, partners and technology tools. They can unlock the potential of global teams, whether they directly employ them or not.

Collaboration technologies have given rise to radical new ways of working and brought the prospect of truly dynamic and responsive virtual teamwork tantalizingly into view. Organizations can harness the skills, experience and energy scattered across their workforce and focus them on individual projects. With the rewards on offer including reduced costs, enhanced creativity, better decision-making and more knowledge exchange, the stakes are high.

Yet even with the latest technologies at their disposal, many businesses struggle to keep their virtual teams on track. Breakdowns in intentions, workstreams, responsibilities or deadlines can have a domino effect on trust, motivation and engagement, leaving them to fall far short of expectations. It's not easy to keep people motivated and engaged when they may never meet up in person. How do you give your organization, people and virtual teams the best shot at success?

The activated organization

We have been privileged to work with many of the world's largest and most complex organizations. What our experience has shown us is that the ability of a digital human-based organization to become truly activated is largely determined by the ability to get three things right:

- *Decision-making and executing*
  The ability to make smart decisions and execute well through smarter ways of working and use of technology.

- *Engaging and motivating*
  The ability to engage and motivate digital humans to participate in work in a meaningful way.

- *Learning and getting to the next level*
  The ability to sense and respond to change and rapidly build capability so that organizations and their people evolve to operate at increasing levels of sophistication.

Getting these right means getting access to almost unlimited expertise, skills and knowledge on demand. It fits with the way people want to work today: flexibly, digitally and connected.

The 12 principles of the activated organization

To achieve this, we propose 12 principles across these three areas that provide a framework to activate organizations in the digital age.

Decision-making and executing

- The spine: how to organize decision making and knowledge making.

- Build together: how to collaborate and create alignment across virtual teams.

- The organization of one: how to design work around people's lives.

- Add-app-ability: how to apply an app mindset to organizations.

Engaging and motivating

- Theatres of work: how to create and use an ecosystem of connected environments.

- Build beautiful things: how to build trust through delivering excellence at every step.

- Playing games: how to use gamification as a major lever for engagement.

- The power of small things: how to lead in the digital world.

Learning and getting to the next level

- Targets and the mirror: how to use feedback for navigating.

- Always learning: how to deliver transformational learning at scale.

- Meaningful alternatives: how to define and share a future that people want to step into.

- Turn it on: how to create a movement and activate the power within it.

In each chapter that follows we explore each principle in turn and we ask for each:

- Why is this principle important?

- What can we learn from history and what is happening in our world today that informs what organizations need to do in the future?

- How can we implement these principles to transform our organizations from the inside out?

SECTION 2:

DECISION-MAKING AND EXECUTING

4.

THE SPINE

'It is better to create than to learn!
Creating is the essence of life.'

Julius Caesar

We explore how our organizations have become complex labyrinths of knowledge and how knowledge informs decision-making. We also discuss why quality decision-making for large groups is difficult, especially when working in virtual teams, and how to create better processes to support them in using digital tools. We reveal what we mean by the spine and why it is fundamental for digital transformation.

The power of the book

Julius Caesar is credited as the inventor of the spine of the book. This small change revolutionized the way information was processed and transmitted. It is said he required his scrolls and papers to be bound at the edges as it was easier to transport them. The spine had the added benefit of providing easier access to the information and apparently aided his decision-making on the battlefield.

In a scroll, access is strictly sequential; in a book we can be less linear and jump straight to the page we want. The invention of the spine meant that information could now be indexed, accessed at any point and cross-referenced. It was perhaps the first random access memory system. The spine's ability to provide not only detailed information but simultaneously retain access to that information's context (i.e. the entire book) is not something we have bettered since, even within the digital realm.

Scrolls would remain in use until the 6th century AD, but the creation of the spine is regarded as one of the most significant milestones in history and in the evolution of knowledge and communication.

Perhaps the biggest revolution in the organization of information in recent years has been the shift to hypertext and tagging as the dominant form of encoding and retrieving knowledge. It represents an equally phenomenal advance. Coded by Tim Berners-Lee, hypertext enables words, phrases and references to be coded and linked to others stored elsewhere. It essentially defines a specific address for any piece of information anywhere. This great web of knowledge would lead to the Internet, letting us surf information, ideas and concepts in a way we now regard as commonplace.

However, it brings with it a set of new problems. Access to so much information can be overwhelming, requiring continual organizing and contextualization to be useful.

The organization of knowledge

In 1768, the first printed edition of the *Encyclopædia Britannica* was published. It was always intended to be a complete anthology of every kind of knowledge and covered seemingly everything from aardvarks to zombies. Encyclopaedias have been published since antiquity, but the innovation of Britannica was to compile essays by recognized experts on related topics, then organize them alphabetically. Previous encyclopaedias only listed concepts and definitions in alphabetical order, much like a modern dictionary. Demons would sit near dentists and Mozart would always follow a monsoon.

Britannica brought a new way of navigating knowledge. One that contextualized information and brought common concepts and ideas together. Britannica has also moved with the digital times: the oldest continuously published reference source in the English language published its final print edition in 2010 and is now available exclusively online.

Connected to everything, everywhere

The advent of digital has brought new formats for the sequencing and organization of knowledge. Google and other search engines have radically changed the way we access information. They provide a mechanism that enables anyone to find information online quickly and easily. These systems are self-organizing. The intelligence built into their search algorithms means that they not only find information but also continuously add indexes to their own database of connections. In doing so they track what's popular and what's most relevant, making our online searching feel ever more natural. It's not surprising that Google is one of the world's most valuable companies. It allows us to make sense of the labyrinth of knowledge.

But what about in a work or research situation where we are at the other end of the knowledge spectrum – the creation of new information? Work has become a continual process of generating and organizing a steady stream of information from both inside and outside the organization: from the data generated by a plane carrying people from one city to another, to the information that flows throughout manufacturing and supply chains, or the tracking of services in call centres. Our working lives are inextricably involved with the creation of new data and the synthesis of knowledge. Even when we are making real-world objects, these days much of the work is done using computers.

We remember the shift to the connected organization distinctly and specifically. There came a day in the 1990s when our freelance employees started to use email addresses provided by AOL or Hotmail. It required those of us inside the firm to start dealing with these private emailers from outside the closed confines of the organization. Before that we had simply used email to communicate internally with each other. The toppling of this wall was significant and we remember well the conversations at the time as to whether we were permitted to access external emails on our internal systems. Of course, it didn't take long before lawyers required us to attach long disclaimers to each email, but the shift had been made, the impermeable membrane had been pierced.

Enter the labyrinth

Organizations today are in many ways like labyrinths – a maze with multiple pathways and many dead-ends. They are also continually evolving and reconstituting themselves. How do digital humans navigate and make decisions effectively in such a world – and how can their organizations make it easier for them to do so?

In Greek mythology, Ariadne was in charge of the labyrinth of sacrifice that lay below her father's palace. In the famous tale she fell in love with one of the victims, Theseus, and saved him from certain death either at the hands of the Minotaur or from wandering lost in the labyrinth. She did so by giving him a ball of thread with which he could record his path as he progressed and therefore find his way back out of the maze.

When in a labyrinth, as Theseus discovered, a successful strategy is to mark with a thread or to draw on the wall on one side as you move through it. In this way we are always able to find where we are in the maze and move forward with the certain knowledge that we can find our way back. As Hansel and Gretel found, dropping breadcrumbs is another way, although unfortunately, one at risk of being lost to the birds.

We are, of course, not limited to using a ball of thread when looking to navigate a labyrinth of knowledge. Instead of adopting a single path or a tightly defined system like a dictionary, argued Umberto Eco, the Italian writer and a luminary on language in the post-modern age, we can use the flexibility of an encyclopaedia. He described how the labyrinth of knowledge is broader and more complex with infinite possibilities. For Eco, it is a sphere of ideas, which has no centre, periphery or exit. It can be structured, but never definitively.

Knowledge then becomes a network of interlinked relationships. We may not reach a specific answer, but we gain the freedom to pursue a never-ending series of connections and meanings. It is the same way search engines and wikis have brought order to the Internet, as hyperlinks open up a library of knowledge and ideas. (These ideas of exploring and connecting a web of all knowledge were also explored by Hermann Hesse in his 1931 novel, *The Glass Bead Game*).

Organizations have always created new knowledge, simply by virtue of their information processing. However, today's organizations are a mass of programmes, knowledge and data in continuous development, with the consequence that information processing is no longer a by-product but the modus operandi. The 'red thread' for these organizations is the ability to put into practice the methods and tools that enable them to document, reference, create and map knowledge as they progress. For organizations without such a focus, hard-earned knowledge will be lost. They are doomed to remake everything again and again on every occasion. In this day and age, that is an expensive error.

Knowledge and decision-making might once have been power when they sat at the top of organizations. Today, competitive advantage is gained by enabling every individual to find their own path through the labyrinth of information: to learn quickly, understand the big picture and make good decisions at every level.

In a simple or autocratic organization, decision-making is easy. Someone at the top decides – for better or for worse. For complex, connected organizations, decision-making needs to involve many stakeholders with access to many sources of knowledge. Why does group decision-making tend to be difficult and how can it be optimized? How can virtual teams in particular, collaborate and make decisions effectively?

Why is group decision-making so complicated?

"Would you tell me, please, which way I ought to go from here?"
"That depends a good deal on where you want to get to," said the Cat.
"I don't much care where–" said Alice.
"Then it doesn't matter which way you go," said the Cat.
"–so long as I get somewhere," Alice added as an explanation.
"Oh, you're sure to do that," said the Cat, "if you only walk
long enough."

Alice's Adventures in Wonderland, Lewis Carroll

In our experience, many organizations find decision-making and maintaining alignment with large numbers of stakeholders spread across multiple locations not only difficult but incredibly time intensive. This is typically due to a combination of too much, insufficient or poor quality of available information along with suboptimal decision-making processes. The results of this are:

- *Insufficient information and poor quality decision-making process*

  With neither the appropriate information nor a good way to work though the information available, a group will become 'lost in the fog', randomly jumping from one idea to the next, not knowing what they don't know. The equivalent of a family choosing a holiday by randomly throwing darts at an unlabelled dartboard, not knowing what each segment represents.

- *Too much information without the appropriate decision-making tools or process*

  This leads to stasis or information overload with the team often moving around in circles. Our holiday-choosing family are surrounded with travel magazines, recommendations and possibilities, but have no idea how to use all the data to which they now have access.

- *A great decision-making process but insufficient context and knowledge*

In this situation, any decision could take the group down the wrong path. The group is directionless. Our family could work extremely efficiently towards a decision to go to a beach in Greece, but not be aware that it will be cold and raining at the time they want to go.

A good decision-making process

Good decision-making can therefore be expressed simply as the effective processing of information to a desired outcome. For large teams and complex decision-making, this will depend on the level and quality of information available, the number of potential options explored and the number of stakeholders who will influence, be involved in or be affected by the outcome.

Here is a critical understanding that we have discovered from working with large, complex teams online: good decision-making is a constructive process. That is, the best decisions are made by groups building something together. A good decision-making process therefore optimizes a group's ability to work information in a collaborative way. To navigate information, the process needs to be flexible, allowing a group to explore, build, test and iterate in an appropriate manner, at the appropriate time. This ensures the group is not 'answering the wrong question' and is engaging all stakeholders in the outcomes. By establishing an objective to build something together and working through a process to achieve that, online collaborative groups will find context becomes easily understood and things will get done.

Successful decision-making is also a creative process. Consider the process of writing a song, for example. Until the tracks are laid down in the studio, the musicians, songwriters and lyricists often have many different ideas and may struggle to communicate them to one another. But once the song begins to materialize, the process becomes necessarily collective and the many ideas collapse into a single version, which will be packaged for distribution and consumption.

This doesn't mean that the artists are completely satisfied with the fidelity of the finished product compared to their individual original visions. Constraints of ability, budget, time and other factors will have modified the song numerous times and the end result may be quite different. This doesn't imply that the first half of the process should exclude collaboration either. Collaboration is a necessary component of every stage. So is independent work. It is the reconciliation of these two modes of working that impacts the quality of the outcome.

Decision-making online

One of the main barriers to extending decision-making and working together online is trust. The reason face-to-face meetings and events are powerful are because they accelerate the building of trust between people.

Think about how a local neighbourhood operates. When we would like someone to do work for us, say for a tradesman, an accountant or a cleaner, we ask our friends and neighbours to provide a personal recommendation. When asked, the vast majority of people will recommend someone they have worked with before or have already met and know. Whilst there's a reasonable chance of this person being a good choice, it's hardly providing a full scan of the available market. As humans we typically give more weight to personal contacts and experiences rather than statistics.

The question is how can we build the level of trust achieved in the local neighbourhood, when working virtually – and do it quickly? Trust comes from spending time together and problem-solving together. Natural leadership and processes tend to emerge when a group has a significant task that the members of the group find urgent and challenging. However, when we are online, the same contextual and unspoken cues that we can see and are accustomed to are not available to us. Imagine constructing some flat-pack furniture whilst a group of friends try to help over the telephone. It doesn't work. We need the right tools to enable a similar level of experience for working together online as when face-to-face.

For a large, connected organization, two challenges exist. First, managing and navigating a constantly evolving body of knowledge – maintaining and using the libraries of information that sit on servers or within the brains of their people. Secondly, enabling virtual teams to use this knowledge collaboratively to make good decisions.

The digital spine

'We cannot solve our problems with the same level of thinking that created them.'

Albert Einstein

In any complex system, a structure is required to organize and sequence tasks. In our bodies, genotypes give us our building blocks. These take shape in the form of phenotypes – our individual characteristics such as the colour of our hair or how tall we are. These characteristics evolve over time.

Spines have also evolved as a way of helping us organize. From the spine of a book to the spine in the human body, they are pathways or threads along which decisions are made and information is transported, grown and synthesized over time.

Digital working is about creating and using information in many forms, visual and written, and about making decisions. It is not enough simply to connect individuals together by providing video communication or access to joint folders. Collaborating teams need to have a clear pathway of activities and tools to help them work on ideas together. As the team moves forward the pathway needs to evolve dynamically, updating all the time. Without clear visualization of the work to be done and a map of the way to get to the outcome, it is almost impossible to navigate or to build common understanding. Teams need accurate and up-to-date feedback and tracking, so they can see where they have come from, how the work is organized and what they need to do to achieve their goal. We call this dynamic pathway a 'digital spine.'

A digital spine is the sequencing of activities and documenting of knowledge and decision-making over time that supports and guides the work of a team or large group of people. It is the binding through which all the knowledge resources, people connections, tasks, activities and technologies can progress together.

Practically speaking, we believe this is a new class of software or app functionality. The digital spine of a programme, for example, could be provided by a single online platform that provides all the resources, tools and learning required.

Digital spines can also be viewed as dynamic recipe cards for project teams. They contain a pre-designed set of activities and provide a visual representation and structured methodology for all involved. Much like how word-processor software contains formal letter templates that the user adapts to suit their needs, a digital spine can provide templates of tasks to get things done.

Let's take as an example a project for designing a new operating model for an organization. A classic, consulting-led approach would be for an external project team to run a series of face-to-face workshops to understand who the stakeholders are and then map the current and intended future state of the operating model. They are likely to bring some best-practice experience and examples for the client to consider, along with some frameworks (process charts, organizational diagrams, prioritization matrices etc) that help guide the thinking. Depending on complexity, the project is likely to take several months, thousands of air miles and many hours out of the client team's regular working day to attend the various meetings and workshops.

We can describe this approach to operating model design with a simple work-flow template or a recipe card. The steps might be: stakeholder mapping, current-state analysis, requirements gathering, future-state design and recommendations. Now, let's bake this know-how into the technology, remove the consultant delivery team, and move the entire project online.

To do so, we need a series of apps. Each app has an appropriate framework built into it. There will be an app for prioritization, an app for process mapping, one for brainstorming, timeline planning and so on. We refer to these as 'decision apps.'

Now the entire project can be sequenced on a digital spine with each of the steps in the process represented by a decision app. For example, let's say the team needs to accomplish a work step that requires it to brainstorm and then prioritize a set of ideas. Rather than hold a physical workshop or have a meeting via conference call, a decision app enables each team member to add and prioritize ideas in their own time. The software dynamically maps the prioritized ideas onto a matrix, which appears on the team's digital spine as the next activity to complete. They can then set a time to access and work through the results together.

A library of these decision apps forms a set of building blocks from which many recipes can be created. These support a wide range of workflows.

Teams can work together asynchronously and can easily adjust and add activities as required to a digital spine. Instructions for how to use each app are provided within the software. No consultants are required to move from one stage to the next. The technology automatically moves the team through the process. Equally, each member of the team can be working on a number of different transformation projects at any one time without losing track.

To ensure the team is working with the latest thinking, the software platform contains up-to-date learning content, best practice examples and access to online experts that support the team in designing and achieving a quality outcome.

Designing digital spines

Digital spines combine knowledge and process. They have three elements that resolve the issues of dynamic knowledge management and decision-making for virtual teams:

- A curated knowledge library that provides relevant learning and examples. In our experience, these are seeded with existing knowledge and best practice and then extended over time by the project team as they add their own research and examples. This allows the knowledge base to grow, remain relevant and inform future projects.

- A robust decision-making method that is made up of a sequence of defined steps. Each step is a decision app with a specific methodology built in. The sequence may be defined initially by an internal team or provided by external experts. It is re-usable by multiple teams working on similar types of project.

- A digital transformation platform that creates an adaptive journey and is flexible to the specific needs of a project. It provides a single point of access for each team member to the project spine, the supporting knowledge resources and the social tools to interact with team members online. Leading examples of such platforms provide a personalized interface that presents the user only with the activities and information relevant to them.

Such digital spines with 'recipe cards' now exist for a large number of transformation requirements. From future state visioning activities to designing new processes, building roadmaps, engaging people or even building capability, they are available for organizations to use at a fraction of the cost of a traditional, externally led programme.

This approach also makes for a lean and cost-effective implementation. By using methodology encoded within digital spines and decision apps, organizations can plug in expertise as required. Teams can facilitate the process themselves with minimal or no external support. These tools provide automatic documentation – the thread through the labyrinth – and real-time information on progress and results. We believe that this is the future of global transformation and it will change the game for the traditional delivery model of change, especially in management consulting.

In practice: smart events for strategy design

Events, either on site or virtually, are often the point when a spine comes most sharply into focus. Events determine how effectively an organization can bring together a team or a group to collaborate, strategize, engage and implement.

In one example, a leading change management consultancy wanted to align its global leadership team to achieve significant growth by harnessing the opportunities presented by big data, digital and analytics. They needed to bring together the top 150 leaders across the globe, agree their 'big bets' and define a plan to roll out the strategy. The only problem was that they didn't have the time for everyone to travel to be together.

Our solution was to provide a 'smart event'. Delivered through our SmartLab transformation platform, it provided the event design, delivery and post-event documentation. The Smart Event took the form of two three-hour facilitated online sessions, each with around 150 participants. The sessions contained a structured design process with a sequence of decision apps. The event was supported by a multi-disciplinary creative team of business experts, artists, film-makers and designers, that coordinated every aspect of the event delivery. We provided facilitation to guide the discussions, along with documentation in the form of visual scribing and reportage.

Through this process, the client was able to collaboratively re-invent their change management practice.

Conclusion

Organizations now act like living systems. As with any living system, change is constant. Even at the cellular level in our own bodies, we are not the same person we were yesterday.

For organizations, change can no longer be controlled or led in a top-down, mechanistic way. As they become ever more networked, they become like a labyrinth of connections, pathways and knowledge. A new ordering approach is required. By using a digital spine, virtual teams can access the tools they need to participate in collaborative decision-making, build trust and generate alignment.

Specific methodology with apps containing built in work-flows can be provided to support virtual teams in their work. Encoded with decision-making, collaboration and knowledge-sharing know-how, these tools are replacing the traditional model of externally led, process-based consulting.

Through digital, everyone can now have meaningful involvement in designing solutions. Decisions and outcomes can be easily documented and visualized. The question for organizations now is how far they go in taking a virtual approach to transformation without having to fly people around the world or bring in external resources. The opportunity is to shift to a model where organizations can use digital tools to transform themselves.

5.

BUILD TOGETHER

'Necessity is the mother of invention.'

Plato

> This chapter looks at the role of digital in collaboration: the need for a shared language of collaboration and for digital tools that make our collaborative work meaningful and satisfying. We also introduce our proven approach for building together with virtual teams.

In the 5th century BC, Plato believed that the most effective form of democracy was one where every citizen was involved in policy decision-making. At that time, the democratic assembly of Athens met on the hill of the Pnyx, which simply didn't have enough space to accommodate the estimated 40,000 citizens who were entitled to vote. The citizens didn't have the time to always be present to deal with the volume of decisions that needed to be taken. Plato's dream of democratic involvement by all was frustrated by logistical impracticality. His solution became the representative democracy we recognize today; have people vote for representatives who can vote in their place.

Now, after two-and-a-half millennia, that dream could be entirely realized. The gift of digital technology is that the virtual hill of the Pnyx is as large as we wish to make it. If we choose, we can empower every person affected by proposed change to have a voice, not as an afterthought, but as the conversation is happening.

The opportunities we have in the 21st century have a dimension that Plato didn't envisage. The power of the digital human goes beyond voting. Way beyond. The tools available to us mean we can participate in building together wherever we may be located. It is this power that is transforming global culture and shaping our society.

The power of building together

Throughout history, the power of building together has catapulted societies to enormous wealth and influence. One example we love is Venice in its golden age.

In the 14th century, the Venetians re-invented ship building. Already a maritime powerhouse, they built the Arsenale Nuovo (New Arsenale), an enormous manufacturing site for building military and commercial vessels. At the time, it was the largest industrial construction site ever made. At its peak, the Arsenale employed almost 16,000 people.

In the Arsenale, the Venetians radically changed the process of ship building. They created a far more efficient frame-first system (rather than hull-first) and re-invented construction by creating the first moving assembly line. They used the waterways to move the ship galleys through each stage of development to the waiting workers. At the time, elsewhere in Europe, shipbuilding would take many months. At the Arsenale, up to one hundred ocean-going, three-storey, wind and oar-powered, vast cargo-carrying triremes could be in production simultaneously and completed at a rate of one per day. They worked at a scale, volume and speed unimaginable to other societies at the time. Venetians would bring visiting dignitaries, diplomats and traders to view a demonstration, just to remind them of the power of La Serenissima, the Serene Republic.

In order to fund the voyages that went to the East to trade, the Venetians invented the modern corporation. They legislated for corporations and permitted joint investment. They invented modern banking practices to advance loans on the basis of the profitable return of the ship. They used insurance in case things went wrong and they invented modern double-entry book keeping to account for it all. They invented craft Guilds to ensure that knowledge was protected and developed; in order to create the most magnificent objects to trade. All of these practices meant that Venetians could collaborate together for profit.

The Venetians' ability to build together at scale meant that they dominated commerce across the Mediterranean for hundreds of years.

We buy into what we build

If there's one frustration we've heard more than any other when people work together is that their team members 'just don't get it'. No matter how much time and effort is spent on communication, the not-invented-here syndrome seems to be ever present.

Plato, as well as the Venetians, had the right idea. When people are involved in building the outcome together, they can achieve phenomenal results. Furthermore, after many years of working with people from organizations all over the world, we've found that unless individuals are actively part of making the solution, they rarely engage with it. People buy into what they build.

Building something together is far easier to achieve of course when teams can physically work together. The question for digitally connected humans is how can virtual teams work effectively together? How can we bring together all the stakeholders that need to be involved, if they are spread across geographies and time zones? If we do bring them together, will the end result be any better?

Surely, it's impractical to involve so many people with such varied degrees of expertise and experience? It may be hard to believe that opening the floodgates to all doesn't create chaos and a many-headed monster. Many leaders have expressed a similar concern. As Churchill put it: 'The best argument against democracy is a five-minute conversation with the average voter.' Aren't we just advocating too many cooks to spoil the broth?

Working together without being together

Prior to widespread use of the Internet, collaborative work was paper-based, and required enormous resources and support teams. In the 20th century, the mode of working was almost entirely face-to-face. In 1936, Frank Lloyd Wright invented the open plan office for the Johnson Wax organization. It was a factory of white-collar workers and he created beautiful but costly buildings and furniture to support this 'machine'. Later as this style of working environment became the norm, workshops became increasingly important as mechanisms for collaborative decision-making, innovation, design and transformation.

As our organizations spread across multiple locations, leaders who wanted to bring their people together to co-design a solution did so at enormous cost. It has meant a lot of costly flights, hotels, and consultant-led workshops, usually involving vast amounts of flip charts and post-it notes. Programmes also struggled to be implemented properly, once the teams of people were no longer together. The question remained – how do we ensure implementation of change in a cost-effective and impactful manner when working virtually? A question we have been working to solve for ten years.

With the technology tools now at our disposal, digital humans are able to collaborate together in teams of all sizes. As we described in the previous chapter, software can now do the heavy lifting of facilitating and documenting this work. There exists a multitude of collaborative white-boarding, process-mapping and brainstorming tools and apps. We are now at a point where we are able to imagine an entirely different set of techniques for enabling very large-scale collaboration across time and distance. What we need are the processes and language that allow virtual teams to collaborate in a way that engages everyone and gets rapid results. We've learned, just like the Venetians Guilds, that we need to organize ourselves online around different types of work. We need access to different resources at the right time in the process. Most importantly, we all need to be able to identify where we are in the process and what's coming next.

There's strong motivation to work in this manner. The global organization that can get strategic change implemented quickly and thoroughly with the least disruption wins the day. The key to this is to have a common collaborative language that enables us to chart a course together, and to navigate the entire journey.

Design thinking

Design thinking is an excellent process language for this task. As the name suggests, it is essentially how any designer works. It's complementary to the scientific method of discovery through experimentation. The difference is that designers think 'backwards.' They start by imagining the outcomes they want to create for the user or customer. From there, they bring the solution into reality through iteration with each version closer to the final goal. Designers make wireframes, lo-fi prototypes and models throughout the process to make things real, so they can test what works and gain feedback from real users. They may start the process with deep research, based on scientific findings, but at the end of the day, the outcomes required are what drive the decision-making.

It's a proven method that engages relevant individuals and viewpoints throughout the process of developing a new or improved product or service. Design thinking is made even more powerful when it is used to shape collaborative work.

One story that demonstrates the power of scientific research working alongside design thinking comes out of a multidisciplinary group at the Royal College of Art (RCA). The challenge was to design something new that would assist young people on the autistic spectrum. Psychologists, medical experts, designers, engineers and families working with these challenges were all on the team. Not an easy task. The science provided them with insights. For example, they discovered research that proved that feelings of safety and control were paramount for children on the spectrum. These scientific insights, when coupled with the design process, focused on the qualitative outcomes. The involvement of the families led to the development of a range of clothing and coats that had 'huggable' characteristics. Pulling on a drawstring enabled the wearer to be hugged by the coat, bringing about a sensation of safety. Further scientific research confirmed that the clothes had a significant impact on enabling autistic teenagers to feel safe and be better able to control their responses to different situations.

Design thinking, in tandem with scientific research, enables the synthesis of ideas and application of fact-based knowledge by collaborating groups.

The problem of virtual collaboration

Transformation work in large organizations today is becoming more like that of a modern design or film production studio. Diverse teams with different skills, knowledge and practices need to work together to create new products and services. It's similar in many ways to how movies are made. Scenes are filmed or graphics created at different locations around the world, each with a different crew. The soundtrack is created in another studio. The special effects and editing are then completed somewhere else. Each of these teams possesses specialist equipment, software and a professional language that enables them to share their work and collaborate in making a single product.

The challenge that many businesses face when implementing change is that the outcomes aren't as tangible as a film, a game or a piece of furniture. They are often abstract and difficult to visualize, for example, a financial product, a new way of working or a different organizational model.

Consider the following scenario: a team from across different geographies of an organization needs to work together to design a new recruitment process. A traditional method may be for a small team, all recruitment specialists, to come together for a series of workshops. They draw up all the existing processes, understand what is similar, what challenges exist and what currently works well. The team then designs a superb new process, fully streamlined and efficient. So far, so good. However, now the real problems begin.

The new recruitment process no doubt requires new technology to support it. Various departments across the organization need first to understand what the process is, then they need to be trained to use it. At the same time, perhaps new suppliers are involved, leadership responsibilities change, the list goes on. Meanwhile, the people who preferred their current way of doing things are really not keen to adopt this new approach designed by 'some experts in a dark room'.

In the end, perhaps leaders decide to force through the changes, mandating the use of the new process. Or perhaps it all takes too long, other priorities emerge, technology changes and the whole idea is put back on the shelf, after much expense of time and money.

What's required is a way for large virtual teams to develop solutions together, involving a wide range of stakeholders throughout the process, so that everyone involved has a part to play in building the outcomes together. In other words, design thinking for digital humans.

So, what are the digital tools that we need to build together when working in such large or virtual teams? What new methods will enable us as digital humans to construct today's equivalent of the complex ships of the Venetians in their Arsenale Nuovo?

Collaborative authoring

Collaborative authoring is a design-thinking method for virtual decision-making and alignment that we have defined and applied since the start of our journey. It enables virtual teams to develop, build, test and iterate together in a similar way to when they are face-to-face. We have been developing this approach now for several years.

Collaborative authoring uses rapid, iterative cycles to optimize and accelerate how information is processed, problems are solved and decisions are made. We reduce risk by working through scenarios and building prototypes to test in the real world. We are thinking like designers to engage more people in building together.

It is a process of 'thinking by doing.' In our work, we have found that new ideas are best created through the process of making something, for example by creating visual images, 3D prototypes and lo-fi prototypes. Ideas that are visualized first are more likely to succeed because they cut through ambiguity and reduce complexity. Working with visual sketches and mock-ups are the most powerful tools to overcome misunderstanding and ambiguity for virtual teams. As far as possible, we bring in timely external viewpoints and expertise to encourage a creative flow through which more can be achieved than anyone thought possible. The practice of doing the work together builds mastery across the team.

In exploring options and taking decisions, the process of building moves forward through continuous cycles of iteration. Groups move through phases of scanning the landscape of information, defining the question as it really presents itself, generating ideas and alternatives, then creating scenarios, prototypes and narratives to test against reality, before synthesizing the feedback to upgrade to the next version.

For example, a team might work together online, both simultaneously and individually, using apps specifically designed to support their work, which are sequenced over time in a digital spine of activities, as described in the previous chapter. This guides the team through a design-led process. They might start with brainstorming and visioning, then scenario testing and prioritization of requirements, followed by solution design, implementation planning and so on. Much like the traditional approach of using post-it notes and flip charts, the best digital apps visualize and organize the work as it happens, even with everyone working from a different location.

By building something that can be tested in the real world, even if it is a virtual representation, we create a third point of reference that we can all stand back from to observe and learn. It means we can be hard on the model and not on each other. Differences of opinion are focused on improving the work and on the desired outcomes. Making improvements means we simply need to shift the model rather than tear down the ideas of others. If opposing views exist, we test both simultaneously to see which one best achieves the desired outcomes.

Creativity is often the process of eliminating options. As the French writer of *The Little Prince*, Antoine de Saint-Exupéry said: 'Perfection is achieved not when there is nothing more to add, but when there is nothing left to take away.'

Usually the opposite happens. The tendency is to add more detail, extra features and try to satisfy all conditions. In reality, the goal of being hard on our solutions is to find ways to make them better by being simpler. The more we can cut, the more efficient we can be in conveying our message. Less is more.

Collaborative authoring means thinking like a designer. In particular for virtual teams, the approach releases the potential of the people, increases the quality of the product and reduces the time to get it made.

How to think like a designer and build together

'It's through mistakes that you actually can grow. You have to get bad in order to get good.'

Paula Scher

Here are nine ways that help us think like a designer in resolving challenges and making better decisions.

Bring the right minds together from the start

In the late 18th century, a few extraordinary minds in Great Britain transformed our world. The original Lunar Society or Lunarmen gathered together regularly for dinner and discussion. The Lunarmen were mostly centred around Birmingham, the industrial hub of pre-industrial Britain and they would meet at every full moon. They were led by Erasmus Darwin, a man of extraordinary intellectual insight. His famous work Zoonomia contained the early thinking which led to the development of his grandson Charles Darwin's ideas on the evolution of the species. Others included the entrepreneur Matthew Boulton; James Watt the engineer who harnessed steam; Joseph Priestley, who discovered oxygen; and the potter and social reformer, Josiah Wedgwood. Their debates brought together philosophy, arts, science and commerce. The 'Lunarticks' built canals and factories, managed world-class businesses and ushered in the Industrial Revolution.

Designers bring in many different viewpoints throughout the process to understand what is really required. This often requires going outside the usual sources. Solutions may already have been found in other disciplines or in other industries beyond our own. Teams with diverse sets of skills and knowledge find stronger and better solutions. We look to bring in as many potential groups of stakeholders from the start and keep them involved throughout.

Focus on the question not the answer

A high-quality design process begins with a deep understanding of the context. We spend the time to understand the current situation, why the work is necessary and important, who it will benefit and how. A full understanding of the context helps to demarcate the problem and to get to grips with the core issues to resolve.

In parallel to exploring the context, we need to scan and understand from research what has already been tried, what possible solutions exist, what challenges have already been faced.

Online platforms make it easy to form communities of interest for sharing ideas, knowledge and resources, both within the organization and from outside. These function like the Venetian Guilds. Digital tools make it far easier to gather and synthesize opinions and ideas from all over the world. Automated tools make visualizing massive data sets not only possible but quick and readily accessible.

All those who need to be involved in addressing a challenge within an organization are now able to engage meaningfully, regardless of location. They can use digital tools to explore the context and identify the right questions to ask. Insights are achieved by everyone involved by 'learning by doing.'

Define the terms of art

When a group of people get together they can design a building or a bookcase, an algorithm or artwork, they can create a skyscraper or have a cocktail party. The difference between each of these interactions is intention and language – the set of terms and terminology that codify their intention, determines the outcome.

Imagine the simple task of making an omelette without shared terminology. We're going to make a gooey-yellow thing. Let's put the heavy thing on the hot thing. We'll then open three of the oval things and mix them up with a mix-them-up thing. A shared understanding of the terminology to be used is the first step in a collaborative creative process.

Every discipline has its own unique language. Transformation itself is no different. We use words like systems, processes, outcomes, culture, measures, agile, scrum, goal and lean to name a few. Not to mention the hundreds of unique TLAs (three letter acronyms) every organization has. If we bring a team together, even from the same business area, at the start of a working session, we will ask each person to define their understanding of key words relating to the topic in their context. These form their terms of art. For example, the words growth, result, knowledge and culture each mean something completely different if we are talking about microbiology rather than learning. Every time we work on defining the terms of art with a group, we see a range of different responses. How can we work together on the same problem if we are working with different meanings for the same term? How much more difficult is it if we come from different geographic, theoretical or academic backgrounds, each with its own language?

We've seen heated arguments among team members, caused by nothing more than a lack of common definitions for the terms of art being used. In one particular case, the team could not agree on the vision. One group felt the vision needed to be more ambitious, inspiring and bold. The other group wanted the vision to be practical and reachable. In the end, the issue was not the elements of vision, but about what would happen by when. The ambitious-and-bold group

77

saw their ideas being realized in five years; the other group had a one-year time horizon in mind.

Taking the time to establish an understanding across all teams of the terms, words and language to be used enables groups to move forward quickly and with clarity. New realities require new terms: think of quantum physics, or machine learning. Such terms also need defining and adding to the group's lexicon.

Take a look at our own terms of art listed at the end of this book – which ones do you agree with and disagree with?

For virtual teams, establishing a common language is paramount. Apps exist that enable a group to build and maintain an agreed vocabulary. Even simple online exercises are helpful in exploring and defining the terms of art before the work begins in earnest.

Build a 'there'

A key part of design thinking is to create a powerful description of the future state, right at the very start of the process. It should be as complete as possible with all stakeholders involved in the development. Think of how architects work with their clients to design a new building. They will create a detailed sketch that visualizes the completed structure, adding as much detail as possible to every element. They might even create virtual models of the building that allow the client to explore as if they were walking through it. This way, the client can clearly see, experience and challenge what will be built before a single shovel hits the ground. An architect will create a number of different solutions in parallel, that each contribute to the development of the solution.

When working virtually, we often bring in a visual artist to help teams record the ideas using drawings, models and images. We have developed an app that enables everybody to see this visual record grow over time. One effective process that quickly builds alignment is to ask everyone to create their own vision of the solution – and actually draw it. They then photograph and upload their ideas to share with the team. Through discussion of each person's work, the best ideas and the challenges emerge. The visual artist captures and synthesizes the ideas from the discussion as it happens, to create a single picture that represents as full a representation as possible of everyone's input. The net effect is a set of ideas that have tackled the problem from every single individual's perspective. We have used this process with hundreds of people. There is something powerful in asking people to solve a problem using methods other than writing or rhetoric. Drawing a picture of the solution enables us to articulate complexity and relationships between ideas and take them to the next level.

Iterate together

Working iteratively can be a highly productive process. However, it's just as easy to get it wrong. In the process of creating a stage play, the writer develops a first draft, which is then improved by the contributions of the director, the actors, the set designer, sound designer, and the whole creative team. The actors will have insights into their characters in ways which the writer may not have imagined and may then choose to use. Directors likewise will have a way of telling the story that adds or clarifies in their mind what the text is trying to achieve. The finished work may be quite different from what the writer first imagined: for better or for worse. Think of how many times one of your favourite books didn't work as well as a movie or when the simplest short story is turned into an epic adventure on the big screen.

A good iterative process requires the work to move forward constructively. Each version resolves problems of the earlier stages. It's a balancing act to make sure that too many conflicting ideas don't confuse or diminish the result, whilst still keeping people engaged. Typically, it's about making sure the original vision remains front of mind throughout. This is one of the jobs of the digital spine.

Online tools exist that enable the development of ideas from many places simultaneously such as participatory media sites (e.g. blogs and wikis). Project management tools and other social software enables very large groups to work together on documents and projects simultaneously. With better data speeds and increased familiarity, video conferencing and collaboration software is becoming

ALIVE: DIGITAL HUMANS AND THEIR ORGANIZATIONS

commonplace. They make it easy for people to have far richer conversations with others at different locations from their desktops.

Test in reality

'No plan survives first contact with the enemy.' A piece of military wisdom derived from a formulation by the 19th-century Prussian military commander Helmuth von Moltke and equally true of solution design and decision-making.

The best way to test an iteration or model is to apply it to a real scenario. Scenarios or design challenges stretch the thinking, enabling us to test our ideas in reality to see what will work and what won't. For example, in designing a new sales process, a scenario might focus on how different customer groups might respond or how it will work for different product types. A design challenge might include: How can we implement this in half the time? How can every part of the process be automated? How can we make this more accessible to everyone?

Working with scenarios to test ideas often brings new thinking into reality. In 1936, H. G. Wells created his film *Things to Come*. The way in which the film predicts a new society and attempts at space travel is remarkable. When one watches it today it's shocking how prescient it is. Have we created the future Wells imagined, because he imagined it and filmed it?

Digital tools make developing scenarios and testing through data and user experience easier than ever. Managing the feedback is vital. We use apps that keep a visual record of progress and results, so any advances are quickly assimilated and any corrections or adjustments can be made.

Use story as well as science

Strategy is not just about having a purpose, measurable results and a plan to get there. Millions of PowerPoint slides setting out the most beautiful new strategies have been written and have proved entirely pointless. They may be well received by leadership teams but they are then never implemented. Why? Perhaps because there's no engaging narrative. No story. Without an engaging story, only the strategists will buy into a strategy. No one else in the organization cares.

The storytelling and discussion promoted through online channels, when created within forums that enable ideas to develop in measured ways, are leading to one of the greatest waves of innovation in our history.

We are in an age where we are stimulated with new ideas as never before. Children are making sophisticated movies and sharing them via YouTube and other channels. These ideas are being tested by the hardest judges of all, the public, and sometimes even emerge fully formed into the movie industry. Incredibly powerful storytelling tools are now in everybody's hands. From discussion forums to interactive film, it is far easier to bring new ideas to life and deliver them straight to every individual's desk in a consistent way at zero cost. The creation of such prototypes and narratives catch the imagination of all those involved.

Making media has become one of the main ways in which collaborative authors can generate and visualize reflections on the past, present and future to bring new ideas into focus. We talk more about the power of storytelling in the chapter 'Turn it on.'

Exhibit and show

Often the most difficult part of the creative process is presenting the work. Putting forward our work for the consideration of others is an exposing and challenging task. The act of showing has always been important for making things. It is the point at which we expose ourselves to the critique of others.

One of the single most important moments in the development of the Industrial Revolution in Britain was the Great Exhibition in Hyde Park, London. A brainchild of Prince Albert, it brought together under one roof every major industrial and commercial artefact from across the British Empire. Victorians came in the thousands to look, learn and exchange ideas. Not only were the public exposed to the inventions of the Empire, engineers and scientists sought to solve the problems introduced to them by the Great Exhibition. It was also a huge commercial success. The profit from the Great Exhibition was used to create a grand new building intended for ongoing promotion of the sciences and the arts. Queen Victoria herself named it. Originally named the Central Hall of the Arts and Sciences, on the day she walked into the vast space, she surprised all by announcing without consultation that it was to be called The Royal Albert Hall in honour of her beloved and departed husband.

There is no irony in the fact that in our work, we have collaborated with and tested many of our ideas at the RCA, one of the world's greatest post-graduate design schools, that sits alongside the Royal Albert Hall.

The September Issue documentary revealed the processes behind the making of the most important and biggest Vogue magazine edition of the year. We learn that the team is able to achieve their vision because they visualize and plan the entire edition on the walls of the Vogue offices. The fashion industry is another example of where the entire creative process, from concept to prototype to fabrication, is achieved through continuous cycles of showing and exhibiting. How can this be achieved online? We have to use collaborative tools that enable us to see the big picture in context, as well as being able to work on the minutiae.

It is important to recognize that performing and showing is a vital part of the process. Unless our ideas meet with reality, they can never be tested and used. We advocate creating opportunities to exhibit online throughout the design process and developing complete iterations for show and feedback. Virtual teams can exhibit by making media, giving online presentations or hosting a virtual symposium. Virtual reality can make these experiences even more visceral. We recommend planning these specific event horizons with a real audience, whether sponsors, leaders, colleagues or users. They define an endpoint for each cycle of work and a goal for the team to work towards.

Document throughout

How we create knowledge, use it and edit it is at the heart of the digital revolution. The digital knowledge bases we have built over the past few decades are enormous and ever expanding. In particular, knowledge has become highly media-based. Children (and adults) tend now to turn to YouTube rather than Google to learn how to solve a problem. They want to see how it is done, rather than read about it. Think of how many photographs the average tourist takes on a single trip, all stored in the cloud. Every famous monument in every corner of the world has been photographed countless millions of times. We digital humans seem to have an insatiable desire to document and learn from almost every new experience we have.

In organizations, as teams and individuals move through cycles of creativity, design and production, they create new knowledge at every step. This forms a narrative of the journey of the development. It is not just the end result that is catalogued, but the iterations along the way are also stored for future referral. 'Version control' — originally applied to software development — is now the bane of every project manager's life with multiple versions of every file, document or image appearing from everywhere. As we discussed in the chapter 'the spine', knowledge management is becoming a key survival skill for all organizations.

Paying attention to the knowledge environment in which virtual teams operate enables more powerful decision-making and speeds up the work. Ideas and outcomes can be documented in every format (text, video, sound, handwritten, photographic and the web) for further reflection and learning. Together these knowledge objects form a rich contextual story of the outcomes that teams desire.

Conclusion

Digital not only provides opportunities for groups to communicate more effectively around the world, it also provides us with the opportunity to create together.

People engage in what they build, and the process of building media-based artefacts, which is an iterative, creative and engaging process, enables teams and individuals to align.

Within digitally alive organizations, decisions are now being reached, innovations are being created and knowledge is being sourced through multi-disciplinary working. The whole organization and its networks can engage in an intensive dialogue facilitated by many collaborative technologies.

Digital unleashes our ability to be constructive. Visual media and the creating of things enable powerful decision-making, whether for services or physical objects.

Using collaborative authoring, a virtual team can be highly effective in making decisions and developing new solutions. Working this way is beyond rules, micro-processes and mechanistic styles of working and can lead to highly-motivated groups of people achieving extraordinary outcomes.

Through the cloud, project teams with the right tools can design solutions and solve problems as easily as if they were face-to-face. We can work through rapid design cycles, accelerate solutions, save time and travel costs and ensure successful implementation. By following a structured path online, with common terminology, virtual teams can now deliver a project as if they were designing in close proximity.

The digital reality enables us to solve complex problems and launch solutions into the world in ways that involve more people than ever before in history. With the right set of tools and methods, digital humans are already solving previously unimaginable problems.

6.

THE ORGANIZATION OF ONE

'In order to change an existing imagined order,
we must first believe in an alternative imagined order.'

Yuval Noah Harari,
Sapiens: A Brief History of Humankind

This chapter is about re-wiring the way we work and a shift in the social contract between employers and employees. It is about designing organizations so that they are tailored around every individual involved with them. Whether providing a more personalized customer experience or a radically flexible employee experience, leading organizations will differentiate by providing greater degrees of personalization for everyone. They will need to because systems or organizations with greater diversity, less homogeneity, faster change and more openness, tend to win in the competitive stakes.

Gathering together

Advances in civilization have always occurred when we gather together. It happens through the stories we have shared around a fire, the tribes who formed around the harvest, and in more recent years, mass urbanization as millions move to cities in search of work and new opportunities. As Yuval Noah Harari described in his book *Sapiens: A Brief History of Humankind*, our success as a species can

85

be attributed at least in part to our ability to gather together and cooperate in large numbers.

We are currently experiencing one of the most profound shifts in history of how we gather together. We are moving rapidly towards far greater flexibility and choice in terms of where and how we live and how work is done. As the fibre optic cables that forms the backbone of the Internet is rolled out, technology is reversing the trend of urbanization, revitalizing our smaller towns and villages and reduces the necessity of commuting.

Social media and digital mobility means we are now gathering together in entirely new ways. The community of friends and colleagues we interact with every day may not even live in the same country, never mind the same town. We are becoming a society of digital tribes.

Digital tribes

A tribe can be defined as a specific group within society with a common culture, language and set of practices. Typically, they also have recognized leaders. In the past, the tribe we were part of depended predominantly on geography and background. Groups formed for protection and growth with like-minded people nearby. Now, we form tribes around our interests and expertise and with people who are similar or complementary. We also form tribes for strength, support and access to knowledge. We move in and out of these tribes throughout our lives depending on our needs.

With the advent of digital, we are able and free to join as many tribes as we like, wherever they are in the world. The barriers to entry are knowledge-based and success in the tribe has a lot to do with how much you are seen to positively contribute. Active participation is key. It's a lot like being in a teenage gang. In order to be a member of a skateboard tribe, you've got to be able to skateboard, but you also have to pitch up, hang out and contribute to the tricks your gang can perform. Digital humans participate in physical and online communities in all aspects of life: to learn, play sports, share ideas and tell stories. We often feel more affinity to these new tribes than the traditional links of family or neighbourhoods.

Digital tribes can quickly build scale and have great power, particularly when focused on a specific service or interest. Leaders, whether political or in business are often playing catch up because of the shifts in demands and expectations that these tribes cause. We have recently seen some of the world's largest companies lose billions of dollars in value following a swing in tribal opinion, in response to a political event or a single post or tweet from a celebrity.

Throughout our lives we digital humans can build a portfolio of skills, knowledge and experience that is portable and re-usable. Some of us choose to work with multiple organizations in parallel; deploying our time and talents as required across a multi-tribal set of allegiances. Others are members of professional tribes, such as medical personnel. These days, fewer of us are aligned to and working for only one organization (or mono-tribal). Today's organizations are required to work and engage with individuals from multiple tribes simultaneously and need to be aware that for these employees, their banner is potentially only one of many around which they gather.

Leaders now find themselves managing large and diverse groups of people, with multiple teams working remotely and in many different ways through different digital platforms. The identity of a single organization becomes more fluid and diverse as those who work within it change over time. What do leaders and their organizations need to do to continue to attract the right skills and people to their cause? How do organizations remain competitive, diverse and unique in a market when ideas and processes are rapidly shared amongst them?

How do we want to work?

As we described in our look at some of the big trends, automation is already changing the nature of work and replacing a number of existing roles. In the past, factories have been at the forefront of using robots to speed up and automate work. Now, in every type of business from airlines to retailers, people are being replaced with bots. From burger-flipping robots, to customer service chat-bots the machines aren't just coming, they are firmly here and they're serving us our coffee.

In 50 years' time, what will our descendants think about how we spent most of our waking lives in the early 21st century? Will our grandchildren ask: 'What is work? Isn't that something the robots do?'

For those not suffering the indignity of automation, digital provides a great deal of freedom for employees and employers. At its best, some can live the dream of creating work for themselves, from wherever they may be in the world. We know trainers who skype in for their classes from a beach in Thailand, IT programmers who work for half of the year and ski or surf for the rest. Businesses are able to tap into their expertise on demand, wherever these experts are located. Many national health services already supplement a shortage of local resources with doctors from across the country or even from other parts of the world. These virtual doctors provide consultation via video conference. Online appointments are often more convenient for the patient too. Flexibility works both ways: employers can access a much wider pool of talent and individuals have greater choice in how and when to work.

A side-effect of radical flexibility is the removal of some of the worker protections established over decades of industrial relations. We have already seen the excesses of the gig economy and zero hours contracts leading to complete job insecurity. We believe that it is inevitable that employees and knowledge workers will band together in tribes of their own and demand a fair social contract with their employers. Take for example one of the trail blazers of the gig economy, Uber, and the recent ruling that its drivers must be classified as workers and therefore enjoy the same rights as other employees. As the machines take over many of the traditional roles at work, organizations will need to pay more and more attention to what and who they are optimizing for. If a system optimizes only for its customers, at the expense of its workers, it may find that there is a backlash.

A new employment experience

What kinds of employment experience do digital humans want? Can we really design work to fit around our lives? How do we balance an individual's desire for flexibility with the needs of large organizations to maintain order and gather their people together effectively?

Digital is bringing personalization to all aspects of our lives, from the clothes we wear to the media we consume. More and more, our expectation is to have what we want, when we want it. In a world that can be configured to every individual's needs, digital humans are now bringing similar expectations into the workplace.

As such, a new relationship is emerging between organizations and their people. In the competition for the best talent, organizations are required to offer a far more tailored employment experience. People in the same organization may have extremely varying contracts: from flexible and ad-hoc contracts to full-time employment, entirely remote working to fully office-based, and everything in between.

In the more developed nations, human life expectancy is increasing, as is our health span. As people choose to work longer and later in life, organizations will need to cater for an increasingly diverse workforce. Employers could potentially have more than half a century between their youngest and oldest workers and therefore will need to cater for multiple generations simultaneously in the way they recruit, develop and engage.

We expect that there will be negotiation of terms of work and retirement ages with individuals in conjunction with their tribal groups. Younger people may choose to experience several different careers, potentially re-training as they move between each one. In addition, the combination of longer lives with better health will lead to older people taking personal decisions on when or whether to formally retire or merely shift into another phase of flexible working that better suits their lifestyle. For example, we work with a global network of leadership coaches, almost all of whom are over 50 years old and semi-retired. Experts in their field, each coach essentially writes their own contract in terms of when and how they work. These coaches work almost entirely via video conference and use online platforms for administration. Global time zones mean that those wanting to work early in the morning or late at night can do so, keeping most of their day free for other activities.

For many organizations, the challenge lies in how to manage this tendency towards radical individualization at scale. How can we provide a far more personalized employee proposition, whilst still managing the workforce in a consistent manner?

We believe the employee experience at work will be become as vital as the customer experience that organizations have been focused on for many years. Employee engagement levels have remained stubbornly low. Surveys typically see only 50–65 percent of respondents saying they are engaged in their work or organization. Often, this is lower still for flexible and remote employees. The extent to which organizations can offer a personalized experience of working, one that is organized around the work not the office, will become a big differentiator in the employment market. Those that can do so while at the same maintaining a shared sense of purpose, culture and knowledge will be able to draw on the best talent and remain unique and competitive.

The organization of one

Imagine the scene. Society does not use money. It is not needed. The economy is planned so efficiently that every individual has all their basic requirements met. People do the work they need to, based on their individual expertise. They form social groups of complementary skills to live and work. People specializing in particular activities gather together to learn from each other and optimize the way they work. The exchange of skills and knowledge across these groups continually increases social wealth for all. Local government ensures abundance for all by re-distributing resources to locations where facilities and products are not available. Are we describing a utopian scene some 20 or 30 years from now as digital becomes even more interwoven in our lives? No. We are referring to the Andean civilizations that have existed in what is now South America for thousands of years and, in particular, the Incas of the 15th century.

The Incas had one of the most successful economies the world has ever known. Their system of people working together based on their individual skills created so much wealth that the Spanish conquistadors were amazed by what they found.

The Inca Empire was a blend of many cultures, languages and peoples. The economy was based on a barter system of goods and labour. The concept of the *allyu* was at the heart of the Inca's success. Each *ayllu* was a small community gathered around a parcel of land. Working together, each individual contributed with his or her labour. Work was divided into regions – agricultural *ayllus* were based where land was most productive, other *allyus* focused on ceramics, road building and textile making according to where the skills resided. The government collected and re-distributed any surplus. In return for their work, each individual had access to free clothing, food, healthcare and education.

The Inca Empire was essentially designed around the skills of each individual and the resources available to them. The Incas generated enormous wealth and achieved incredible things. They built more than 18,000 miles of paved roads in some of the most difficult terrain in the world, suspension bridges across wide canyons and the astonishing Machu Picchu.

The Inca civilization was incredibly sophisticated for their time. They recognized the power of applying the individual knowledge and across multiple tribes for the benefit of all.

We believe that in the future, as in the past, our skills will be bartered and exchanged between individuals and our now digital tribes, much like they were in the communities of the Inca villages. As the machines take on many of the roles we humans would prefer not to do, one possible outcome is that people will have more choice about the nature and the amount of work they perform. For those who choose to work, they will do so with organizations that offer a compelling employment proposition that is relevant and meaningful to them. We will choose to be allied with organizations that are designed around us. This is a concept we call 'the organization of one'.

Can an organization design an employee experience tailored to every individual and be able to deliver this at scale? What will make an organization attractive to the digital humans in the future? What are the elements of the 'organizations of one'?

Have a clear and shared purpose

The clarity of purpose and the identity of an organization's brand will have an increasing impact on its ability to attract and retain the best talent. Diverse groups working from multiple locations can easily dissolve, unless there is a compelling purpose, a common professional language and common way of working. Organizations with action-oriented purposes make it clear that everyone has a role in delivering it. These are particularly impactful. For instance, for a pharmaceutical company this could be 'curing cancer' or 'eradicating disease'. It's a shared purpose that inspires everyone from the research scientists to HR professionals.

As the Incas and modern social media groups alike have shown, the strength of a tribe's purpose and culture along with its ability to engage diverse groups of people within it, directly impacts the ability to generate results. Consider how quickly a protest can be organized online or a crowd empowered to problem solve when focusing on a specific outcome.

For example, the toy manufacturer Lego, is responsible for probably one of the best examples of digital tribal working we've seen. Suffering from stagnation, the company launched Lego Ideas to engage Lego's passionate community of users in helping them to innovate. Through Lego's own platform, users can design new products. Lego is able to test these ideas with the community in parallel. Any user can submit a design that other users are able to vote on. The winning ideas go into production and the original creator is paid a one percent royalty on the profit.

Having a clear purpose that it is shared amongst the entire tribe, everybody who works with or is a customer of an organization, draws people together and provides focus.

Provide personalized employment experiences

From our research, we have found that many people do not want their work based around the morning commute or regular office hours. They want complete flexibility. Many want to be able to have multiple projects with several organizations simultaneously. At the other end of the spectrum, many people continue to require and prefer a fixed desk and a highly structured work day.

Companies are already experimenting with how to personalize their employment experience. For example, Netflix, LinkedIn and Virgin offer their staff unlimited holiday time. Many companies offer highly tailored rewards and incentive packages. Intelligent talent management systems recommend courses or roles to individuals relevant to their needs to help further their careers. Data analytics can be used to provide a holistic view of the impact of many aspects of work from the use of a staff car park or day-care facility to the career paths and the knowledge networks that exist across an organization. Smart organizations will use this data to design employment propositions that are more relevant to the individuals and tribes they engage with.

Working with digital humans requires a different mindset and a high degree of trust. Personalized employment is not just about being able to work from home or more holiday time. It requires careful design and planning that considers the work environment, the nature of the work, the digital tools available, development opportunities, how people choose their work, as well as rewards.

Engage with digital tribes

As we have always done as a species, we operate from the safety of our tribe. Whether our families, social groups, or groups built around a professional specialism, these are the people we always come back to and in many ways define and give us meaning. Organizations cannot ignore the tribes in which people operate and need to actively engage them as part of their ecosystem.

Many digital humans carry with them, on their own digital devices, the sets of tools and apps they need to get their work done. Just as carpenters have a toolbox of hammers, saws and screwdrivers, each digital tribe has its own shared toolbox of digital content and software tools. Individual members of the tribe need to be able to connect securely and seamlessly with their employers' existing technology systems.

One of the key ways that digital organizations can differentiate themselves is by providing access to a competitive suite of digital tools and apps. We address this specifically in our next chapter add-app-ability.

Tailor communication on demand

No one size fits all when it comes to communication and collaboration. We have found that organizations are struggling to get the communications balance right. With the number of channels and tools increasing, the opportunity for confusion and communication chaos increases. Many organizations need to dramatically improve the style of communication and the channels through which they're delivered.

Outside of the office, digital humans have access to media on demand. The everyday experience of information, news, documentaries, sports and even gossip is that information is available at our fingertips in whatever format we desire: text, image, podcast, movies and more. In contrast, many organizations are struggling to keep up. Investment is required in platforms that serve relevant and personalized messaging to individuals at a time convenient to them.

We know many employees of large organizations who have practically given up on email. Is this indicative of a trend? The sheer volume of emails they receive on a daily basis is unmanageable, especially with the current tendency to include everybody's manager and teammate on every message, just in case the content of the message is missed. Unless a specific enquiry is sent and addressed directly to them, they might not even read it, less still respond.

Conclusion

The organization of the future is proving to be a complex network of relationships and of people with vastly differing employment contracts, needs and experiences. Organizations now need to work with many different digital and physical tribes who each have their own purpose, language and tools to get things done. Organizations will differentiate themselves and compete on the quality of the digital platforms, experience and apps they provide to their tribe to get things done.

The digital organization of the future will not only promote radical collaboration, it will successfully enable multiple and diverse relationships with individuals. The notion of value is being extended by the digital realm. What we as individuals contribute is shifting to something that enables us all to tailor our work to suit our individual needs and requirements. No longer does one size fit all. On the contrary, it's a case of all shapes and sizes for all shapes and sizes.

7.

ADD-APP-ABILITY

'The architect must not only understand drawing, but music.'
Marcus Vitruvius Pollio

This chapter is about a radical shift in the way work is
governed. Digital now enables us to programme and adapt
our organizations in a dynamic and modular manner.
When we are able to programme the world around us,
organizations operate less like highly tuned, classical
orchestras and more like jazz bands: free flowing and
inventive – ready to improvise and adapt. We introduce
the concept of add-app-ability, describe how this idea will
define the digital organization in the future and how to
put add-app-ability into practice.

The Vitruvius within us all

Beautiful and complex buildings have been constructed from simple
modules since antiquity. Even now, more than 2000 years later, we are
surrounded by the classical forms of architecture that we inherited from
the ancient empires. For example, the Roman classical architectural
system that we still use today was first fully described by Vitruvius, an
engineer who originally specialized in designing siege weapons for the
Caesars before turning to civil construction.

In his *Ten Books of Architecture* written in the 1st century BC,
Vitruvius argued that all buildings should follow a repeating sense of

proportion based on three principles: strength, function and beauty. He devised a modular system, based on the semi-diameter of each column, which could be followed across the full extent of the Roman Empire, maintaining the symmetry of classical forms.

Vitruvius's sense of proportion inspired the architects of the Renaissance who rediscovered and elaborated his system, creating 30 modules against his original six. His works also prompted Leonardo da Vinci to produce one of the most influential drawings in the history of Western culture: the Vitruvian man. It placed the dimensions of the human body within a circle and square from which proportions, ratios and measures were determined. The enduring quality of these theories is that they described a language of proportion that could be scaled across empires.

As digital humans, we modularize in every aspect of our lives. From ready meals to 15-minute fitness workouts, from the apps on our smartphones to our smart homes. We organize our days into as many discrete activities as possible, governed to the minute, so that we make maximum use of our time. The open modular ideas that sit underneath the app development platforms are infecting many other areas of organizing. By opening up the development of apps and creating toolkits, the app store providers have created a scalable, modular system not unlike that designed by Vitruvius. The millions of apps that are produced encode new ideas, algorithms, services and product offerings within a huge ecosystem that generates masses of unforeseen functionality. These apps then evolve and compete within their various domains. Those with the best combination of interaction, design, functionality, usefulness and support, win.

Building blocks everywhere

Modular thinking is everywhere in the modern world. For example, take the modern-day construction industry. Back in the early 1930s, the Empire State Building broke all records for speed of construction and was completed in under two years. Now, buildings are literally fixed together from a set of prefabricated parts, in a matter of weeks.

In 2015, China's engineers erected a 57-floor skyscraper in just 19 days using a modular method.

You may have heard the story of the three-hour house from 1983. To revitalize San Diego's then flagging construction business, a competition was set: to build a complete house in under three hours. Two teams of 300 workers created two three-bedroom houses in just two hours, 52 minutes and 31 seconds. Perhaps not the best model for every construction job, but it demonstrates the power of modular working.

Run out of bedrooms at home and want to use the extra space in the attic, but don't want months of mess and inconvenience? No problem. Specialist companies will now provide a ready-made modular unit that is lifted straight on to an existing house. Fitting time – two to three weeks. One of the most extraordinary things we've seen on the motorway is a complete four-bedroom house on the back of a transporter. Presumably the owners were tired of their view – or their neighbours – but obviously not their home.

Inside our homes, our world has become modularized too. The Scandinavians are masters of modular thinking. Homes around the world are now filled with modular, flat-packed furniture that can be assembled following (fairly) simple instructions. Cost effective, resilient and with a good eye for design, firms such as Ikea have ignited our passion for prefabricated living. Modularization in production engineering permits new factories to be set up that mass produce new products in a fraction of the time it took in the past. Sophisticated organizations in numerous industries use this kind of modular thinking in the way they manufacture new products and services. From medical devices that can be 3D printed to chips for technology devices.

The ideas of modularization gained ground in the 20th century, at first in military applications and then in domestic production. Buckminster Fuller, the American thinker, made a significant impact after the World Expo in 1967 brought his Geodesic domes into the public domain. His impact on engineering, modularization and standardization has been huge.

We have found that modularization can be applied to almost every aspect of the way organizations manage themselves and conduct change. Modularization isn't about putting in a single large computer system for everyone to use, as was the case in the last 20 years. Now a far more agile infrastructure is required, with individuals and teams being able to use the most appropriate tools for their work.

Bring your everything to work

In the previous chapter, we described how leading organizations will design tailored employee propositions to attract the best people. We believe that the same is true for the apps and technology platforms that will define a particular tribe. Beyond contractual terms and flexible benefits, the work and technology platforms organizations use will need to be configurable and adaptable to accommodate the needs and tools of different tribes. Failing to do so will lead to frustrated people and reduced ability and appetite to get work done. The quality of the app environment and the speed at which it adapts will play an important role when it comes to which organizations thrive and which don't.

One example of this in recent years is BYOD (bring your own device), where employees are encouraged to bring their own laptops to use at work, sometimes with a contribution to the cost of the device. The problem many people find is that even though they can now use their own technology at work, they cannot easily connect with their organization's platforms and systems. This often reduces their sophisticated new machines to simply being a fancy email reader or web browser.

With many large organizations, the experience is often the opposite of a streamlined, modular system. The pace of change is too fast for existing systems of management, security and policy. Organizations seem to be losing control of the impact of technology in the workplace. We are aware of many organizations that have invested millions of dollars in learning or customer management systems that are rarely used and now lie forgotten. They have been replaced even before the implementation was completed, by more agile technology platforms.

The advantage of modular solutions is that they allow solutions and services to be plugged in and swapped out, depending on the needs and projects at the time. This approach means that teams can test and learn rapidly, rather than having to fit within a rigid set of existing features and functionalities.

A constant work in progress

Much like the painting of the Forth Bridge in Scotland which used to be continuous, business is becoming a constant work in progress. Its contours are being re-shaped all the time by digital technologies and new ways of working. Traditional organizational transformation, over multiple years, with a clear and final destination, has become outdated. It is unrealistic and undeliverable in today's fast-moving, dynamic environments. We predict that large infrastructural technology solutions that risk becoming quickly outdated will become a thing of the past. Leaders of large organizations we speak with compare the experience of getting their organization to change, to navigating the chicanes of a Formula One race track with a double-decker bus, continuously lurching from one side of the track to the other.

Just like those racing car drivers, leaders of large organizations no longer have the luxury of pressing pause while painstakingly planning and preparing their next move. The old command and control styles of leadership are redundant. Organizations and systems are evolving too rapidly. The digital world requires a more intuitive, responsive, plug-and-play, agile design to meet the needs of the organizations of today.

De-bossing

In the past, doctrine and policy were the mechanisms used to determine how work was done. These militaristic principles included process-led design, top-down management, and command and control. More recently practices such as customer experience, agile and design thinking have emerged as more appropriate management approaches as they empower teams within a set of guiding frameworks.

Teams designing new solutions need to be able to organize quickly around specific projects or outcomes and to have the autonomy to direct their own work. During our work with organizations, we are repeatedly told that the problem is with the middle layer of management. It's not necessarily the fault of these managers. Today, no single individual or even small team of individuals, has sufficient contextual information or knowledge to be able to solve problems fast enough or accurately enough. In light of this new reality, the old order of command and control is no longer fit for purpose.

One of the biggest impacts of digital is that organizations are becoming 'de-bossed' resulting in far fewer levels of management. Technology is accelerating this change as it replaces the traditional functions of management. Digital dashboards automatically report project updates and potential issues. Resource and time-management systems allocate people to tasks without human intervention. Workflow apps and tutorials can be downloaded and implemented by a team with little guidance. The plug-and-play deployment of these digital tools and apps allow organizations to monitor and evolve using real-time information and knowledge in the same way that a smartphone supplier updates the operating system on our phones remotely and automatically. The issue of big brother surveillance and how detailed and transparent these digital reports should be to management remains to be answered.

My digital companion

For better or for worse, instead of a boss, many of us will continue to work in teams and have a digital companion with us. It might be a robot, a dashboard or an app. Just as astronauts have always had digital companions on their spacesuits to provide real-time feedback on their current situation and workflow, individuals will be provided with a personalized digital toolset relevant to their work.

For organizations aiming to deliver on an ambition of digital enablement and modularizing the way they work, focus is essential. It is clearly unhelpful to have hundreds of apps and platforms presented simultaneously. Individuals will need to be provided with or select the most contextually relevant information and tools at the point where they need them. A different set of apps might be brought to the forefront of the personal digital environment depending on the work to be completed.

Each of these apps needs to be thought of and developed as a simple building block that provide relevant knowledge, process, community and feedback to users at the point they need it. In this way, individuals and teams can operate in a simple environment to deliver their work with autonomy.

We can see this in action by returning to the world of music again. Jazz and hip-hop are great examples of how modular thinking and simple building blocks lead to complex and interesting outcomes.

Modal jazz

Released by Miles Davis in 1959, *Kind of Blue* remains the best-selling jazz record of all time. Its startling originality depends on a revolutionary way to let soloists improvise more freely.

In the previous four decades, jazz had operated within the traditional confines of harmonic progression. Each chord built towards a tonal resolution. The musicians at the centre of the development of jazz asked questions such as what would happen if the rhythm section played a static harmony sequence and we let the soloists freely explore the melodic possibilities within each chord?

It was a concept developed by George Russell, a jazz pianist and musical theorist, from the late 1940s alongside his great friend Miles Davis. Russell was fascinated by the progressions of individual chords around which he could construct scales or modes. This would open up new avenues for every soloist to explore. Together, Russell and Davis spent hours in small rooms in New York talking, playing and developing the codes and language system that would permit jazz to erupt onto the global musical stage. Their adoption of a relatively simple set of rules using modular thinking led to an outcome that remains as complex, creative and potent as when it was first released six decades ago.

Hip-hop started in the Bronx in the 1970s. It simply required MCs on a microphone to improvise over the beats from a beat box. It evolved in countless ways, but access to vinyl, a microphone and some deejay mixing equipment was all it took to spawn a cultural revolution. Anyone could participate. All that was required was an awareness of the language of hip-hop and how to use a few simple tools. Nobody needed years of training on a musical instrument to be involved.

Like jazz in the 1950 and hip-hop in the 1970s and 1980s, modular thinking is now transforming how organizations start up, operate and compete today. The same principles are still in play as our value-creating organizations are in the process of being completely reconfigured by modular app sets.

An app mindset

Smart organizations are already beginning to look like app developers. They no longer wait for perfection. They release version 1.0 of a solution in modular form, then quickly test and iterate. They are happy to fail faster and fail better. They are solving problems by building and testing small solutions that can be rapidly deployed at scale. Instead of writing documents that describe the future, change is being encoded into real tools that employees use every day. Experiences, new knowledge and changes to process are built into existing modules and encoded into existing digital tools and platforms.

Constant evolution of the apps we use makes work more effective and enables one organizational tribe to compete better against other tribes. The quality of the apps and the flexibility in the organization is massively important to staying ahead.

This way of thinking can be applied in more than just the way software tools are developed. An app mindset can be applied to team structures, contracting, process design and even the work environment. An organization, whether a manufacturer, retail store or a bank, can configure its ways of working, technology, knowledge and teams like a set of apps that support all of the various tribes across their businesses. We call this approach to work and managing change 'add-app-ability'.

From small acorns

As we have described earlier, unconstrained by legacy systems and ways of working, a new venture with global scale can be set up in weeks and run from a home office or a smartphone. Every component of its business model can be plugged in: software platforms can be licensed on a monthly basis for sales and payments; delivery outsourced to an international courier; and production completed in Asia.

Entrepreneurs can also innovate existing business models by thinking with add-app-ability. We know of local coffee shops have been able to rapidly grow their business through an app that allows customers to place their order five minutes before they arrive. The shops also use the data from the app to continuously improve demand management throughout the day.

The University of Manchester already excels in creating ventures around intellectual property. Now it is creating a lightweight process to pick up the numerous ideas circulating around the campus that could turn into niche ventures within the regional economy. The automation and digitalization of business processes will only intensify the potential for disruptive start-ups and scale-ups.

Add-app-ability at scale

Add-app-ability is not just for start-ups. Global organizations can adopt the same principles in the way they operate. Consider the following real-world examples from our experiences of add-app-ability in practice.

The plug-in expert

Jason is an organization design specialist. After ten years of experience of designing and implementing change in large multinational companies, he now works as a freelance expert, often with several clients in parallel. Jason has developed his own app that contains his main work steps when he is delivering an organizational design project. From research and interviews, to current-state analysis and future-process design, Jason's clever app has automated much of the day-to-day data gathering. He is able to deploy this within his client organizations during his project engagements and so maximize his face-time with senior leaders and to develop strategic recommendations. After the project has been completed, the client continues to license Jason's app to maintain access to his knowledge base and findings whilst the client takes on the implementation themselves.

Encoding best practice

Anita leads a contact centre team for a major subscription-based media company. Whilst much of the day-to-day inbound work is now handled by automated voice-recognition tools and AI 'bots', the delicate task of retaining customers who are looking to leave is still handled by experienced human agents. Anita created a taskforce team of experts to establish a new process to improve customer retention for these teams. The taskforce used a rapid-design approach to build a new app for the contact centre that described specific customer scenarios and brought together all of their experiences into a single and simplified process. The new app can be easily extended as new scenarios are identified. The app and its scenarios enable the team to rapidly train new people who join them.

Working remotely

Meera is a customer-experience designer for an automotive company. Her work is often on the road, but she works closely with the engineers in the design lab who develop and test new prototypes. Meera's role in the design process is to provide field research from different sectors into how customers interact with voice technology. The company's digital platform that supports the design process contains a number of apps, each enabling a specific task. Some assist with data gathering, some are for documenting and linking new ideas, some for recording and tagging media. As Meera works through the sequence of apps, the engineers are able to access her work in real time and conduct sophisticated scenario modelling on the data. If the engineers require additional information or a new research method to be used, they can remotely update Meera's app sequence, which adapts her workflow automatically.

The sandwich shop

A well-known chain of sandwich retailers has an app for supporting each role in the store. Baristas who make coffee have videos and resources not only to show them how best to do it, but also to enable them to contribute to the best practice conversation with their colleagues across the organization. Sandwich makers are shown tips of the trade for creating great sandwiches. The inventory of sandwich types is shown on a daily basis, and easily updated through the app. A simple change to the app ensures that new taste combinations are prepared and launched almost instantaneously across all outlets. Apps also monitor footfall and enable teams to manage timing and planning. They use real-time data about when customers come in to purchase different types of products. Cash management and accounting is built into the app set, providing the store manager with a real-time dashboard about productivity so they can plan accordingly. Teams are always learning and are able to make additions to the app set that supports their work. Conversations continue online between people in similar roles across the organization, so knowledge is transmitted and shared across the functional teams. If a new role is introduced or a role is changed in some way, the change is first prototyped in the app. In team meetings, individuals update their task requirements for the shift (for example, 'make 50 avocado sandwiches') and the app helps them account for their production. These measures are linked to the store management dashboard.

Adopting add-app-ability

Shifting to new technology or ways of working is always challenging. As humans we often tend to avoid change. However, we are programmed to take the path of least resistance. If a new approach is demonstrably able to make our lives easier or better, it will naturally become quickly adopted. Think about the adoption of 3D TV versus on-demand programming. There are several difficulties to adapt to 3D viewing in its current format: buying a new television, wearing special glasses, turning the lights down and so on which have proved too complex for most people to bother with, even though it's more immersive and experiential. By comparison, by installing a single on-demand box or an app, the experience of watching television is transformed within seconds. Our existing television or laptop can now provide exactly what we want: a fully tailored, ready-when-we-are experience. Online shopping is another example. It has become far quicker to click a few buttons than to walk up and down a shopping mall or high street. Often, it's also easier to return the things we buy online than the items we've bought in a store.

When deploying change, our experience is that it is best to focus on making people's lives easier with respect to the things they already do. Adoption will then be far greater and far faster. Everything requires a reason to exist. We will use new tools and adopt new ways of working if we actually need them and if they make our lives better or easier. Essentially, we will change if we have a powerful reason to do so.

In practice: going digital

One of our clients has recently had a big focus on building their own digital capabilities and creating awareness of digital for all associates. The challenge was to provide a worldwide learning and communications campaign that would demystify digital and give associates the confidence to think and work in a more adaptive way. Working in partnership, we created an online platform that engages all associates with the world of digital for their business and the opportunities it brings to the organization.

It tells the story of the new technologies emerging and how teams across the organization are already using digital to change the way they create and deliver solutions, connect with customers and work together.

The platform uses interactive videos to share stories between colleagues about how they are using digital and how it is transforming the culture and ways of working. It promotes learning by providing curated content, enables progress tracking and rewards participation. It builds communities and signposts additional resources.

Applying add-app-ability

From our experience, here are our four key steps to implement add-app-ability within an organization:

- Consider all aspects of the organization across work processes, technology systems, organizational structures, knowledge basis and more. In each area of the business, explore where it is possible to take a modular approach.

  - What can be modularized and packaged into discrete workflows or services?

  - Establish the best way to design, deploy and scale.

  - Decide who needs to be involved?

  - Which digital platforms and tools already exist that can be used?

  - If the change is to be encoded into a software app or set of apps, establish what functionality is required for users to decide, manage, account, measure and learn on a daily basis?

- Institute a process of development and learning by doing. The steps can often be simplified to improve existing ways of working, streamlining as much as possible. Ensure that conversations and chats are built into the apps that enable people in similar roles to easily connect.

- With a set of modular work activities encoded, the next task is to join up all these new tools through collaborative platforms so that they can work together, sharing and visualizing data whilst moving the work through the end-to-end process.

- Make it visual. Ensure that the workflow, resources and conversations are easily understood and made visual. Use video to demonstrate skills. Use peer-to-peer communication to support individuals. Use simple workflow illustrations to make the knowledge accessible. Connect the data generated in the apps to a dashboard that monitors the outcomes of the team.

As these new tools are used, change becomes embedded in the ways of working within the organization. The organization then has the ability to evolve and the flexibility to exist in a state of constant change.

Conclusion

Transformation is no longer a strategy that comes from the top. Instead, it is a constant process of evolution – learning by doing. Through apps and other smart platforms, everyone will have the ability to adapt their organization themselves as they go about their everyday work.

As we design new ways of working and become increasingly mobile, the quality of our digital tools will have a direct impact on the quality and consistency of work. For leaders, access to real-time reporting and management information can make the organization more agile and easier to align, despite having a dispersed workforce.

However, structures must be put in place to manage the change to provide focus and avoid digital chaos. As we become decoupled from a single physical workplace, it is more important than ever to generate a sense of community and belonging.

Instead of just providing a physical office, the workplace of the future needs to provide a digital infrastructure that enables people to do their work wherever they may be. This is about finding the right tools and channels for the organization to provide freedom and flexibility whilst at the same time encouraging participation and engagement. We will address this need specifically in the next chapter.

Ultimately, the goal of add-app-ability is to build the plug-and-play capability within organizations and their people, so that organizations are able to transform themselves.

The shift to a seamless digital working environment is at the heart of being a digital human, technology working symbiotically with humans. Humans learning from their technology and the technology learning from their humans. The embedded code in our apps transmits the governing rules that are required for scale and collaboration just as Vitruvius embedded classical values into his modular forms. Someday soon, all successful organizations will be run this way.

SECTION 3:

ENGAGING AND MOTIVATING

8.

THEATRES OF WORK

'All the world's a stage,
And all the men and women merely players;
They have their exits and their entrances,
And one man in his time plays many parts..'

William Shakespeare,
***As You Like It*, Act II, Scene VII**

This chapter is about how digital has radically impacted our working, living and social environments. In particular, we focus on what this means for our physical environments when we come together and what the implications are for the digital environments we construct around us.

The digital agora

In ancient Greece, the agora was a public gathering place and the focal point of everyday life in the city. Citizens would walk to the agora to talk together, share ideas and solve problems, often practicing in the gymnasium as well. The agora was an important part of life in ancient Greece and the primary forum for promoting debate and discourse. It is at the root of the democratic tradition with which we are familiar today.

Throughout history, humans have designed meeting places to come together for work, learning and play and these spaces provide a focal point for every kind of conversation. Our greatest arenas still house the biggest sporting events and most important conferences, often broadcast to millions of people across the world.

Although we still meet and connect with each other to work and live, the way we do so has changed dramatically in the past decade. Work, as we've discussed, is no longer confined to the four walls of an office building, it can be done everywhere and anywhere. A single physical environment or even a network of multiple offices around the world is insufficient for digital working. We now need to think of our working environments as a continuous blend of the physical and virtual. Digital humans need to be able to move seamlessly between the two.

What are the implications of digital for our working environments? What are the qualities or characteristics of environments that enable digital humans to thrive? How will they enable work to be coordinated across multiple places?

The enchanting port

According to legend, the beautiful city of Lisbon got its name from the Phoenician 'allis ubbo', meaning 'enchanting port.' In the age of discovery, between the 15th and 18th centuries, Lisbon was the main departure point for the Portuguese expeditions that set off to discover new lands in Asia, South America and Africa. In 1497 Vasco da Gama famously discovered a new sea route to India around the Cape of Good Hope. As a direct result, Portugal wrested control of the spice routes from the Venetians and became one of the ruling nations of Europe, turning Lisbon into Europe's most prosperous trading centre.

However, this prosperous age ended suddenly on 1st November 1755, when one of the most violent and longest earthquakes on record destroyed over half of the city's buildings. The earthquake, followed by a tsunami and fires, left Lisbon in ruins. The enchanting port's reign over the oceans was over.

On the ashes of the old, a new Lisbon was conceived by the first Marques de Pombal, Sebastião Jose de Carvalho e Melo. Before 1755, Lisbon resembled a medieval town with small and disorganized streets. The new layout embraced the pragmatic spirit of the age of

Enlightenment and the city reflected a society in which the citizen, the merchant and the bureaucrat took precedence over the crown, church and nobility.

The city was designed to reorganize the social structures of the city and to facilitate commerce. The new town hall and other commercial buildings around the plaza provided the infrastructures for trade. Long merchant streets that connected the main market squares, subtly but directly, made the point that this area of the city was designated for merchant activity. There was no new law or regulation but simply a designation of use through layout and environment. It was a unique concept at the time.

The narrow old streets were replaced by wide, straight avenues, arranged orthogonally to allow for better lighting, ventilation and security. Around these streets, makers' cottages, artists' studios and spaces for production were established with easy access to the main thoroughfares. Ship administrators could work from their 'home office' whilst being just a few streets away from the main port.

Lisbon had become a stage – a theatre to conduct business and trade. It dramatically shifted the way its inhabitants conducted their businesses and their lives. The city was revitalized following a seismic shift to its established routine and reshaped to fit with new design standards and cultural ideals.

The digital tsunami

In the modern world, digital has created a tsunami of tools and devices that are transforming our work and living environments once again. What are the new enchanting places for digital humans we will need to create as a result?

Consider again how a modern film is created today. Hundreds of people from different disciplines work together both face-to-face and digitally. Many of the special effects created are a synthesis of human and digital blurred into one. Scenes may be shot in Croatia and Canada on green screen or in the ocean. Actors' faces and bodies are superimposed onto life-like avatars that move and communicate as believably as their real-life counterparts. These films are then launched with great fanfare at national cinemas and festivals before being consumed around the world in every possible digital format. Modern film production is a state-of-the-art example of how different environments connect to form new realities, new possibilities and create value.

For many digital humans, work begins from the moment their smartphone rouses them from sleep. We check our emails and respond to enquiries before we have even dressed. Each day may require a different location for work; sometimes in an office, studio or factory, sometimes from a hotel lobby or airport lounge, sometimes, perhaps when the children are on holiday – at home from our personal offices. All of these different work environments need to be designed and configured to enable work to be effective, no matter where in the world we are or through which device we connect.

The distributed work environment

To further explore these distributed work environments, imagine a scenario of how a fictional organization, NewShu, activates a global tribe to rapidly design a new footwear product, ready for personalization by customers.

Recognizing a need to innovate their product range, leaders from NewShu visit several design-based research centres to learn about the latest thinking in product design. Inspired by their visit, NewShu sets the challenge to a specialist virtual design community via an online platform. A design team forms across six different time zones with individuals, all working from their personal design studios. Together, they use a suite of online 3D CAD systems to collaborate virtually to create prototypes and solve problems for the product. Workflow is managed so that the work scheduling is fluid and small problems are packaged like tasks and scenarios to be solved with testing and narratives.

Within a 24-hour cycle, people from around the world, access the design, as groups or as individuals, make the changes and present the scenarios to the team who evaluate and decide. At the touch of a button, 3D designs are created and provided to customers for further personalization. Orders are placed and the shoes are produced via micro-batch manufacturing, printed or knitted at a nearby shop, as easily as sending a file to print at a corner studio.

Designers working in their own studios or at home whilst looking after the family do all of their work online. Each workspace is equipped with the tools the designer needs to complete their work: drawing boards, modelling equipment, dedicated software applications. The physical spaces that the teams use seamlessly connect with their online environments.

The example above demonstrates one way in which multiple connected environments can work together to support digital humans in new ways of working. These principles apply as much to service design and change as to innovation in shoe manufacturing.

We have designed work and decision-making environments for many years. We even have a partnership with an architectural firm that enables us to create unique environments for our clients. Through our experience of working with physical and digital workspaces we have identified six primary types of environments that together form a system of distributed spaces for digital humans to collaborate. We describe these below and how they come together to form an ecosystem of connected environments for the newly configured digital organizations. These are:

- **Centres of excellence:** the new palaces of learning, innovation and collaboration. These are dedicated physical environments that can afford state-of-the-art functionality to facilitate the exchange and development of new ideas and solutions.

- **Cultural and community spaces:** these provide a focal point for specific interest groups within society and places that build identity and narrative whilst making and stimulating new connections across cultures.

- **Production environments:** spaces configured to optimize the effectiveness of teams and large groups working together.

- **Social spaces:** these include members clubs, co-working spaces, coffee houses – spaces that informally connect and provide functionality for people to drop in and work or relax as and when required.

- **Spaces for individuals:** the home office, apps, digital companions, personal smartphones and other devices.

- **Shared virtual spaces and platforms:** such as cloud platforms for storing and sharing data, photos, stories and solutions along with dedicated digital platforms that are designed to support specific types of work.

The combination of these environments enable individuals to move between different workspaces, depending on the nature of their work and requirements at any point in time. They form a checklist for organizations when considering the physical and virtual spaces they provide for their diverse populations of customers, suppliers and employees.

Centres of excellence

Just as the *agora* served the purpose of bringing people together, we believe there will always be powerful physical centres. They meet the requirement of our social species for sharing, learning and creating together. To be relevant and attractive, these centres require higher levels of investment and will have far higher levels of functionality than individuals can typically afford. The centres will be the digitally connected temples of the future – temples of learning, innovation and collaboration.

Brand centres that provide an immersive experience for a specific set of products or services allow customers and employees to explore in a non-linear way that is both physical and online. Some state-of-the-art examples are Nike, Adidas, Bayer or Apple. Professional service firms, such as the leading management consultancies are investing in experience centres. Within these spaces, individuals can try, customize and experience the products and services on offer or work alongside experts in an immersive world. They are physical and digital manifestations of the values and culture that the organization seeks to portray. Many organizations also now use the concept of experience centres, both physical and online, to bring to life new ways of working for their own tribe and customers.

Innovation and education spaces are also forms of centres of excellence. State-of-the-art versions of these spaces are specifically designed to bring large teams together to design new solutions or accelerate learning. These centres may contain a wide range of equipment that supports collaborative design work, such as interactive walls and tables, 3D printers, multi-media production kits, editing suites and the like.

Two such centres where we have had the privilege of joining the design team are the Moller Executive Education Centre at the University of Cambridge and the Pontio Centre for Social Innovation at the University of Bangor. We recently spoke with the directors of both centres and asked them to share their experience of creating world-class centres of excellence.

Moller Centre

'When you look at disruption,' says Gillian Secrett, chief executive at the Moller Centre at the University of Cambridge, 'it is easy to think that technology can do everything.'

'Technology is a phenomenal tool, of course,' she says, 'but the atmosphere in which you work remains really important. You can create a huge amount of shift in a living and breathing space. It is easy to forget what you can gain from being together.'

'So never lose the value of face-to-face. The solutions you reach can then be dispersed through technology. It is the blend of the two that gets the best results.'

The space at the Moller Centre is radically flexible. It is designed to facilitate collaborative learning and the interaction of ideas, making the most of open space and bringing in natural daylight. In its workshops, technical support and tools are on hand to help explore strategic scenarios or resolve difficult challenges. Each room has dual projection, magnetic walls and tablets for the group to use.

'We are an environment designed to support creativity,' says Secrett. 'Through accelerated design, we engage in high-energy, interactive working processes, moving the space into new configurations as the project progresses.'

Pontio

These principles are being applied on a large scale at a £50m facility at the University of Bangor, which is designed to support the growth of the economy in North Wales, as well as to realize the commercial value of emerging innovations more broadly.

The Pontio, which means 'bridge' in Welsh, was designed over an area of 10,000m² by one of the world's leading architects, Nicholas Grimshaw. It links the upper and lower halves of the university, as well as connecting art to science and the university to the community.

It has a 480-seat theatre, which can be re-configured for any type of performance, even aerial dance. There is also a smaller studio and a cinema, as well as a 'white box' space (or high-tech immersive environment) for applications such as virtual reality.

On its innovation floor, it has a hack lab (for digital), a media lab (for propositions) and a fab lab (for prototypes), which students can use in developing a venture or which local companies can access to test out their ideas.

'We are looking to democratize technology,' says Pontio's director of innovation, Andy Goodman. 'We are encouraging new sorts of interaction to scope out ideas and then start implementing them.

'Usually, an innovator will have half an idea. They can see it in their mind's eye and will assume they can hand it over, when actually it will probably take two years of effort to be ready for users. We can help fill those gaps in knowledge and understanding. Through our process of iteration and evaluation, we can simultaneously train individuals and accelerate their products.

'Traditionally, universities specialized in depth. Now we are developing the breadth to bring together business, arts, science and engineering.'

Professional services' experience centre

We also worked with a leading professional services firm that needed a responsive and immersive space to accommodate many different client needs. The client wanted a centre that would offer a unique experience. It needed to work with multiple technology platforms and combine multi-media with the latest collaboration and knowledge-sharing apps.

We designed an experience centre that not only has state of the art architectural capabilities, but also includes the methodology that enables groups to use it effectively. It's a place to try and learn, where users are free to test their ideas and safe enough to fail and start again, enabling rapid iteration and development.

This space now constitutes an exciting proposition where transformative ideas are born and creativity is stimulated. It re-invents the way teams define problems and answer big questions. It brings people together to gain new perspectives, generate intent and move forward at pace.

Creating a centre of excellence

Centers of excellence can require a significant capital investment. Sometimes the characteristics of these theatres for learning and innovation require an entirely new building or renovation. Often it can be achieved through the upgrading of existing spaces. This trend can be seen in the massive re-purposing of warehouses and factories, downtown office buildings and ports that is currently underway around the globe. The architectural challenge is to anticipate all the learning challenges and aesthetic expectations that any group who use these spaces might expect. Architects specializing in such spaces bring to life the application of future technologies as well as ways of working.

When successful they also carefully build the bridge for the tribes that will use them so that experience and ideas are able to translate easily back into the real world.

However playful they might be in design, centres of excellence are serious platforms for the future of work.

Cultural and community spaces

From art galleries and museums to co-working spaces and drop-in centres, cultural and community spaces are becoming increasingly woven into society as additional ways to bring people together. In their function, whether run privately or publicly, experiences are made accessible to more than a privileged few. Around the world, from East to West, our cultural and community spaces are increasingly being reconfigured to meet the needs of the mobile, connected society.

In London, one only has to look at the Southbank Centre and how education spaces have been incorporated into its facilities; or the collaborative work environments created at Tate Modern and the Barbican. Cedric Price, the British architect, famously theorized his fun palaces in 1961. Now, these ideas when incorporated with technology, which was a possibility that he had not foreseen, create unique public spaces for sharing, learning and exploring. Sir David Adjaye has also incorporated such principles into the user experience in his groundbreaking work for libraries in Tower Hamlets. He entirely reconfigured the concept of libraries in the digital era by renaming them Knowledge Stores.

The Shed is (at time of writing) currently being built in New York. It will provide flexibility on a grand scale. The Hudson Yards in New York have been entirely reconfigured to support massively flexible working and diverse cultural experiences. Multi-purpose use, fuelled by knowledge systems and technology, is beginning to define our new public spaces from Cape Town to Cairo, from Los Angeles to Beijing. Renzo Piano is creating just such a place on the site of an old electricity generator opposite the Kremlin in Moscow for the VAC Foundation. In Asia, the Thai Culture and Design Centre is another such hub.

It provides a focal point for design-interest groups within society, building identity and narrative whilst making new connections across cultures.

These are more than just the talking shops or the elite spaces of private clubs designed by the Victorians. They are working spaces that enable groups to produce, manufacture, test and explore within a powerful and stimulating context, often surrounded by challenging contemporary artists, exhibitions and curated experiences.

Connected production environments

Connected production environments are dedicated spaces that help us work more effectively with many different individuals and teams, no matter where they are located. These spaces are configured with tools, technologies and furniture to enable a team to complete their work across time zones and distance.

Just like a music producer, today's project managers, team leaders, sales agents, programmers or financial analysts all have specialist tools and knowledge. They typically need to work with a multi-disciplinary team of experts. When these teams come together, the environments in which they work together has a direct impact on their ability to collaborate and be productive. Different types of work may need different tools. Teams involved with data processing may need sophisticated analytical tools. Groups working to improve a service or process may need equipment that makes it easy to draw their ideas and visualize their work.

When designing such spaces, organizations should start first with the functionality required from the space in terms of the kind of work that will be done. Though one-size may not fit all, we advise fitting production environments with a standard set of modular collaboration equipment and technologies such as writeable walls and multiple connected screens for presentation and visualization of data. This provides a sufficient platform for teams to collaborate while producing and fabricating.

Social spaces

There are many forms of social space that support work today. From co-working spaces and pop-up studios, to airport lounges and coffee houses, from private members clubs to train stations. The digital worker of today needs a network of social spaces from which they can operate – as long as it has wi-fi they're ok.

Co-working

Co-working spaces used to be the preserve of the start-up. A wide range of organizations, large and small, now use them to augment their existing office space or provide additional resources for teams. These spaces often have dedicated play and creative areas, as well as areas for individual work, team meetings, virtual meetings and socializing. They might even have a nursery or crèche for working parents. They often excel at forging new networks across different sectors and social groups and can be a hotbed for innovation, especially when connected to a wider pool of resources such as finance, operational support and technology platforms.

Members clubs

Members clubs typically focus on the member experience. These exclusive environments often have lounge areas for casual working but have also invested in additional features not normally found within informal set ups. These might include cinemas, swimming pools, spas, recording studios, even hotel rooms for late-night workers who can't get home. One club in London is known for its hospitality, providing members who need to stay overnight at short notice with a fresh shirt, coffee and newspaper in the morning. These clubs often have reciprocal relationships with other clubs to form a network of national or even international facilities for the mobile worker. Great examples in London include the Hospital Club, the NED and the RSA (Royal Society of Arts). Around the world, clubs are providing a similar level of functionality and service for their members, and global reciprocity enables workers to move anywhere and seamlessly continue the work.

Informal spaces

The historian Brian Cowan describes English coffeehouses in the 17th century as 'places where people gathered to drink coffee, learn the news of the day and perhaps to meet with other local residents and discuss matters of mutual concern'. The coffeehouse offered an alternative to the alehouse and the lack of alcohol made for an environment more conducive to thoughtful discussion.

Coffeehouse conversation was required to be polite and civil. This was one of the cornerstones of these communities. Coffeehouses were also instrumental in the development of financial markets and newspapers. Lloyds of London, the insurance brokers began life as Edward Lloyd's coffee house in 1688. The London Stock Exchange emerged from the gathering of stockbrokers in Jonathan's Coffee House in 1698 who were not allowed into the Royal Exchange due to their rude manners. People from all walks of life were welcome in coffeehouses (although at the time no women were allowed). As historians have written: 'Whether a man was dressed in a ragged coat and found himself seated between a belted earl and a gaitered bishop it made no difference; moreover, he was able to engage them in conversation and know that he would be answered civilly.'

We are witnessing a resurgence in coffeehouse culture. Today, at the informal end of the workplace spectrum, for the price of a cup of coffee it is possible to find a decent Internet connection and comfortable place to work. Coffee shops, airport lounges, hotel lobbies, even shopping malls and fitness centres compete for custom by offering digital workers a functional and comfortable space to work. J.K. Rowling famously wrote the majority of the first Harry Potter novel from the back room of a coffee shop in Edinburgh. Many of today's business leaders prefer to connect with colleagues in these informal spaces rather than the formal setting of a private office. These social spaces will continue to form an increasingly important addition to our working environments.

Spaces for the individual

Many digital humans now have the same or better functionality to conduct their work at home as they do in the office. From secure virtual private networks, they can connect to their office technology infrastructure or cloud services and continue to work as easily as at their organization's offices. With smartphones, laptops and tablets, most digital work can now be completed anywhere.

Home working digital humans have all their creature comforts around them with no commute and can fully flex work around their lives. Research is showing that people who work from home take less time off sick, are more productive (with fewer distractions) and their organization will have improved retention rates (Canada Life Group research report, 2014).

There are challenges with remote working and for long term home-based workers. Loneliness and social isolation can also be factors. Humans, even digital humans are a social species. Environments that force us to work alone, such as the 1990s office cubicle or a home office all the time, are unhealthy and demotivating. When working remotely, we need to make sure we make time regularly to meet with our colleagues in person to avoid such problems. Purely video conferencing whilst useful, is not enough. We imagine, it will become part of the responsibility of managers to make sure this happens, just as smart watches already remind us to stand up and stretch every hour.

Shared virtual spaces

Finally, there are shared virtual spaces. These provide access to tools, knowledge and connectivity with other team members. Think of media and image-sharing sites such as YouTube, Instagram or Pinterest and collaboration platforms such as SharePoint, Dropbox or Google Drive. Organizations have developed their own shared virtual spaces and platforms and also license proprietary cloud platforms for storing and sharing data, photos, stories and solutions.

These digital environments can be adapted to suit our needs and can even blend physical and virtual environments together through augmented and virtual reality. For example, Ridley Scott, the director of Blade Runner, and owner of The Mill production house, has created a powerful and sophisticated management platform that supports the entire online production process.

Qualities of enabling environments

We believe that organizations that are able to provide and connect all of these different types of work spaces will not only differentiate themselves with the employee proposition they offer but also increase the productivity of their workforce.

As we've described, our own business has been entirely virtual since its inception, working with teams from across the world via digital tools. One particular insight we've discovered from this approach, is that the most useful feature of conferencing software is not the video stream but screen-sharing. Being able to directly work on and refer to the same information at the same time dramatically speeds up decision-making and improves alignment. In fact, these days our internal culture requires that at every meeting, our teams work through a common document or tool via screen-share that everyone can refer to and that is updated in real time.

One barrier to flexible and remote working is trust. Many business leaders believe that if their teams are not at their desk, they must be time wasting or being unproductive. Whilst this may be the case for some individuals from time to time, we have found that this is no greater than if those people were in an office. As research shows, overall, they are in fact more productive. Digital dashboards and collaboration software makes participation levels in work more transparent, improving both productivity and the stress levels of a suspicious boss. However, the focus should not be on putting in the hours; the focus should be on the quality of the outcomes that are produced. The role of the leader is to create the environment in which this quality can be maximized.

We have identified eight qualities for organizations to bear in mind when designing work environments for their digital workers.

Stimulating

We respond to stimulus. The environments we work in should stimulate our minds and provoke a response. Whether this is through visual information, interesting art and artefacts or through layout and furniture, environments that do not stimulate, take energy out of work and reduce productivity. Stimulating environments are also ones that change a great deal. Changing art, interior design and a shifting environment keeps things interesting.

Natural

As far as possible our work environments should reflect our natural way of working. Information should be easy to navigate and be presented simply and logically. Interfaces, whether virtual or physical should be intuitive to use, facilitating work rather than, getting in the way. They should be healthy environments that encourage us to connect with fresh air, sunlight and the earth. They should be flexible enough to adapt to our evolving needs.

Production

Environments should contain the tools and technical systems that enable individuals and teams to collaborate in a productive way, regardless of how they need to work. They should allow for different team sizes with virtual or physical breakout spaces. They need to make it easy to build, iterate, document and synthesize.

Social

Our work environments should encourage the spread and discourse of ideas between people. Both physical and virtual environments have different strengths in this respect. Physical environments can bring people together and through proximity, promote socialization and sharing. Virtual environments make it easier to connect together groups from more diverse backgrounds and locations. Both are important when designing for a flexible workforce.

Connected

Our physical spaces and digital platforms must be connected to allow easy exchange of data. Currently, in too many organizations, the experience of working in the office is completely different to working remotely or from a third space. Organizations will need to work to close the gap by bringing greater connectivity between their platforms and places of work in order to be competitive and attract the best talent.

Real-time feedback

Understanding the impact of work requires feedback. Environments can be designed to significantly help in providing visual and real-time feedback. Visual dashboards, the types of apps we described in the add-app-ability chapter and the use of highly visible data, storyboarding or work flow tools help to create sense in the labyrinth of the day-to-day work.

Culture

Any space that brings people together, whether online or face-to-face creates a certain type of culture. When designing such environments, we need to be mindful of the culture we want to create. Do we require a very open and supportive culture? Should it be highly competitive or secretive? Consider the recent problems with online bullying through social media. Without guidelines and appropriate response to unwanted behaviours, any social group can get out of control. Every tribe has its rituals, icons, language and behaviours that define its identity. When we work digitally, these have to be paid attention to in order to ensure coherence and integrity.

Knowledge management

The resources required to get work done should be easily accessible. The work produced should be easily documented, archived and tagged. Algorithms can help, but so too can active knowledge management processes that ensure that work is easily created and communicated throughout the process. Fundamentally, it should be intuitive, visual and a part of the way of doing things.

Implications

Digital has several implications for organizations and their work environments:

- The quality of the digital landscape (tools and apps) provided will have a direct impact on the competitiveness of the tribe.

- Digital organizations will need to combine publicly available technology with their existing internal technology infrastructure.

- Digital organizations cannot consider themselves closed systems and will need to create a competitive and open ecosystem in order to thrive.

- Digital organizations will need to consider how their physical and virtual environments support tribal working.

The value of physical workspace goes up as it becomes more effective and more multi-functional, supporting different types of work in the same space. In the future, rather than being priced per square metre and by location, perhaps the pricing model will shift to the value that can be generated in that space.

A good example is the warehouse in a failed industrial park outside a city. It becomes inhabited by artists, designers and knowledge workers. In time, small ventures are launched, services such as catering and transport emerge to support them. Studios are created, production facilities are provided, and within a relatively short time, that property becomes incredibly valuable. Simply by virtue of the value it is generating. These sites are then packaged and sold to long-term investors. Developers then start to redevelop the housing and build modern apartments and there goes the neighbourhood.

Conclusion

Digital technology is radically redefining the spaces in which we learn, create and work. It is opening up rich sources of knowledge and data, which we explore together as multi-disciplinary teams. It also gives us a powerful set of learning tools to iterate ideas and accelerate solutions.

The distinctions between the classroom, the laboratory, the office and the club are blurring. Learning is becoming central to facilitating collaborations both within the built environment and through virtual networks.

Digital organizations need to pay attention right across the ecosystems of their work environments and design a supportive and productive experience for the digital humans who interact with them.

The Marques de Pombal re-created Lisbon as a machine to support enlightenment principles. Our physical environments, cities, workplaces and living spaces are being transformed by the new codes of collaboration and learning that underpin the infrastructure of our digital age. These physical spaces are now becoming as programmable as our software environments. What will they help us achieve?

9.

BUILD BEAUTIFUL THINGS

'Everything has beauty, but not everyone sees it.'

Confucius

This chapter is about the value of paying attention to quality at every step in the process of making new things or bringing about change. We believe that quality is a mindset that is fundamental to successful transformation. For digital humans, often working from different locations, this additional effort is necessary to build trust and results in better outcomes. Finally, we introduce our model for building beautiful things that anybody can use to be more creative in their work.

The pursuit of excellence

The ancient Greeks had a term *arete*. It means 'excellence of any kind.' For the ancient Greeks, if something was *arete* it was an ideal represented by the most perfect form an object could take. Partly, it was meant to honour the gods, but it was mainly a celebration of all that we, as humans, can accomplish. Quality is very difficult to define, but it usually implies a coherence and integrity of thinking at every level. We feel that most obviously in music. It's clear when it isn't there; it's just as obvious when it is.

The ancient Greeks applied the term *arete* in many different contexts. The excellence of a building, the excellence of a horse going out to stud, the excellence of a person. It changes its meaning depending on what it describes – everything can be excellent in its own way.

Throughout history, leaders have commissioned the most influential artists and architects of the day to create inspiring monuments, beautiful paintings and incredible sculptures. They knew that such things would amaze, move and inspire their people and stand the test of time.

The best it can be

By 'beautiful' we don't purely mean aesthetically pleasing, though of course if something can be visually appealing then that's usually helpful. Like the ancient Greeks, when we refer to beauty, we are talking about it as an essence or as a principle: the idea of making something the best it can be.

If you work with a team of architects to design an extension to your house or a new kitchen, how would you feel if they arrived with scruffy drawings full of inaccuracies and misspellings? How much confidence would you have in their ability to work through the details required to make the project a success and help you realize your dreams?

The reason for building beautiful things, developing with excellence at every step, is to instill a sense of trust in others in respect of what is being developed. In addition, by making each step complete, it can be properly tested to reveal any potential issues.

Digital makes it easier for everyone to apply far greater levels of design and visualization in their work. Rather than just presenting a table of data, we can create interactive graphics with software tools such as Tableau, interactive films with simple-to-use editing software or 3D models of a new supply chain with free-to-use 3D modelling tools. Paying attention not just to the quality of the work, but also the way it is visualized and presented at every step of the way, helps to build trust and engage audiences and users. As the Balinese proverb says: 'We have no art; we do everything as well as we can.'

Build beautiful things. Why build anything else? That said, beauty is in the eye of the beholder.

Beauty and the beast

'There is a crack in everything, that's how the light gets in.'
Leonard Cohen

The Greeks countered *arete* with their theory of the abject, which is that which we find difficult to consider or from which we recoil. Rather than reject it, we need to understand that there is much to be learned from the abject. Within the abject we may find the source of our solutions. When we step outside our usual frames of reference, we have to ask ourselves uncomfortable questions, exploring what we mean by success and how we are going to achieve it.

The abject may not appear beautiful at first, but as we explore and understand it, we may discover beauty and fresh answers within it. Things we may have reacted to as our younger selves we may come to understand as simply another way of seeing the world. The abject may become completely acceptable as we mature and perceive the reality of a larger universe outside of ourselves. Suddenly we discover that there are ideas, cultures and ways of thinking in the world that are very different from our own.

Some may find that disconcerting and reach for their guns, others may find that exciting and reach for their cameras. In every encounter with the unusual, or with things that are beautiful but different enough to warrant exploration or investigation, we will always need to confront ourselves and our own limitations first.

The poo emoji is a wonderful and fascinating example of how an abject idea, one that initially made many recoil, has been entirely transformed into a mascot for an entire generation.

One of the techniques we use in working to improve a solution is to look at it from the opposing point of view. What would happen if it didn't exist at all? What if we made the most simple, lo-fi version possible? When would users find it most difficult to implement? For example, the answer to improving stalling growth in a new market might be to recruit very different people from the current workforce or to cut one's investment losses in a new but failing system and try another way, even if it comes as a short-term blow.

Whatever is being designed, whether financial products, business strategies or computer chips, the outcome will benefit from such scrutiny and become stronger as a result. Paying attention to where difficulties lie and problems exist, whilst working towards making things as beautiful as they can be, helps to make more complete, more robust solutions.

The unfinished masterpiece

In 1883 a young architect by the name of Antoni Gaudí was commissioned to take over the role of chief architect of a new cathedral under construction in Barcelona. The Sagrada Familia, still unfinished, remains one of the most beautiful and inspiring cathedrals on earth, and one of the masterpieces of human achievement.

Gaudí wanted his design to be immensely symbolic, both architecturally and sculpturally. He was inspired by nature and studied places with natural geometric forms. A thorough researcher, he visited the mountain of Montserrat, the caves of Mallorca, the saltpetre caves in Collbató and the Sant Miquel del Fai in Bigues i Riells.

For the Sagrada Familia, Gaudí had a vision to create a style of architecture that drew on his fascination with nature and his knowledge of geometry. He devised an entirely new solution that was innovative, simple, practical and aesthetic. It came to be called Organic Architecture. He designed the interior of the cathedral as if it were a forest. It would have sets of tree-like columns that divided and twisted into branches to support a structure of high vaults. As in nature, Gaudi's columns perfectly supported the overall structure without need for buttresses – a radical innovation in architecture at the time.

However, that wasn't the most powerful example of Gaudi's innovative approach. Gaudí recognized the need to test and understand how his concepts would work in reality. In order to do so he created his most radical contribution to architecture and did something no one had ever done before in history. To test his organic structure, he created a model that had strings with small weighted bags hanging from them.

On a drawing board he attached to the ceiling, he drew the floor of the church and from this he hung the strings (for the catenaries) with the weighted bags (for the load) from the supporting points of the building. His upside-down model used gravity to show him the exact proportions of his concrete columns. Gaudí photographed his model and when inverted, it revealed perfectly the structure for columns and arches that he needed. His model currently hangs in the Sagrada Familia and is an amazing sight, demanding almost as much attention as the building itself.

At every step in his design process, Gaudí worked to make things as real and as complete as possible. He understood that to develop and communicate his ideas he needed to work with knowledge and techniques from different disciplines, mathematics, physics, nature, art and engineering, applying this knowledge in new ways to meet his challenges.

Gaudí kept to the principle of *arete* throughout his design process. From researching and visioning to testing and realizing his work, every step was made as complete as possible. He knew that not only would this make his solution the best it could be, it also helped him to keep his stakeholders and financiers inspired and engaged throughout the project.

But I can't even draw

For many within organizations, the pursuit of beauty will seem counterintuitive and beyond the skills of the people who work there. After all, they are not trained artists, designers and architects nor are they expected be.

That said, creativity is a process that can be taught and is open to everyone. A good creative process makes it possible to bring together complementary skills and knowledge to achieve outcomes the individuals involved could not have done alone. Digital tools are making this easier and more accessible than ever before.

Gaudí was a genius of course, however he was applying a creative process that almost anybody can use to build beautiful things.

How to build beautiful things

Here's how anyone can use the principles of *arete* to build beautiful things.

Explore everywhere

Just like Gaudi, take inspiration from many sources and consider new paths to explore. Study what is already happening both within your area and beyond. What solutions already exist elsewhere?

There are many digital tools available to help research and document our findings. We can explore faraway places; even go inside many famous buildings through online map software. Research tools such as Mindmapper make it easy to find, organize and curate information. We can build digital mood boards of ideas and images with tools such as Pinterest. Remember the principle of working with *arete*: make every step as complete as possible.

In our work, we try never to start from a blank sheet of paper. With the Internet, a quick search will always reveal an existing model, a basis for ideas or a convenient template. Stand on the shoulders of giants rather than re-invent something that has been done before.

Develop the vision

Next start to develop a vision that is real and tangible, as well as one that is bold enough to include many ideas. A vision could be a visual drawing, but equally it could be a statement of intention, a new model or a framework. We recommend making the vision as visual and complete as possible.

It is often helpful to imagine a future scenario in which your solution is already a reality and then to explore questions that define its components. For example: Who are the customers? How do they use it? What is different now by comparison to what existed before? What challenges were faced? How do you resolve them?

137

Beware the slide show

A word of caution about digital tools, in particular, when developing the vision. Be aware of choosing the right form that best describes the work. For example, too often a quick slide deck is the first choice to create, document and share ideas. In fact, nearly ten percent of the world's population uses PowerPoint as their primary communication tool. How many slide presentations have you made or listened to? The problem is that even with interesting images and animation, just using slides is one-dimensional. Research has shown that most people tune out of a slide presentation within ten minutes. There are millions of presentations, expensive research reports and proposals that lie dormant in drawers and in filing systems, never seeing the light of day, never mind actually being implemented.

In today's media-savvy, digital world, management from the top through slideware is ineffective. It has become a lazy form of communication and may in fact be dangerous for organizations. They risk missing the opportunity to create proper dialogue, engagement and quality outcomes that can inspire, engage and excite stakeholders and audiences.

Instead, create a model, draw an image, make a movie, build engaging formats that bring together everyone's ideas in such a way that the whole team can contribute and understand them. How much does the team or outside stakeholders care about the vision? Is it clear enough, powerful enough and practical enough to tap into the passion, heart and soul of the people it's designed for?

Make it real

Without proper intent, the work will never move off the drawing board. Consider how people from different backgrounds approach problem-solving and solution design. Mechanical engineers would think nothing of creating a simple working model that describes and tests their ideas. A rap artist can easily create a spontaneous story that brings to life difficult experiences. A developer can use inexpensive prototyping software to build an app that shows how a new process might work, in a single day. Each discipline has different skills, tools and ways of working.

Too often in organizations today the way we communicate ideas and solutions ignores this type of approach. Like using a single club for an entire round of golf, one size does not fit all. We need to deliver much higher levels of engagement or immersion for digital humans living in a fast-moving media-rich world. Fortunately, digital humans have access to a huge range of techniques and knowledge through apps, social media and personal connections. Scientists can think like artists, sales people can perform like actors, business leaders can inspire thousands, just like the architects of world-famous monuments.

Digital tools are now available that allow anybody to work with similar levels of *arete* to test solutions by making them real. Take for example, Gaudí's painstaking gravity models. Using a software programme created by MIT, designers can experiment and create similar models of 3D structures by cutting virtual strings and adding virtual weights to see how their building changes form. The processes and knowledge that at one time took a lifetime to discover and apply can now be used by anyone with a smartphone and some imagination. Happily, for the Sagrada Familia, when Gaudí's construction plan was tested by IBM in the 1980s, it was discovered that every element of his plan was sound and would stand as required. A testament to the power of nature and human ingenuity.

Digital tools make it possible to transform the way we develop new ideas. Unleashed from traditional presentation formats, we easily work with ready-made tools and alongside experts from other fields to make multi-media and working models that take our storytelling to another level.

Conclusion

By focusing on the inherent excellence of the work and taking pride in every iteration, we can make each stage of problem-solving or solution design as beautiful as it can be. Through this we open up a stream of creativity inside and outside our organizations that will speed up decision-making and fast track implementation. Perhaps through this we will even create something that will last for hundreds of years.

Versions can always be improved in any case. Experienced creators realize that we have to leave space for others to be part of the solution. At each stage, the goal is to combine individual work with the best ideas from other sources. Building beautiful things at each stage of development promotes trust between groups who may be working across distance and time. The unspoken quality and attention to detail transmits across the barriers of culture, language, time and geography and propels programmes forward.

In the same way and perhaps like the Sagrada Familia, an organization is always a work in progress: a continually iterating set of people, products, services, knowledge and technology.

10.

PLAY THE GAME

'We don't stop playing because we grow old, we grow old because we stop playing.'

George Bernard Shaw

In the digital realm, games give organizations and their people a powerful method for teaching, informing and inspiring, as well as having fun.

A love of games

Being human and the playing of games is inextricably linked. They are in the fabric of our species, an essential part of being alive.

The ancient Greek playwright, Sophocles, claimed that Palamedes invented dice in about 1400 BC. However, dice were developed independently by many ancient cultures around the globe. They have appeared in cave paintings. The world's oldest board game, Senet (meaning 'game of passing') dates back to 3500 BC. The exact rules are unknown, but it consisted of a grid of 30 squares, arranged in three rows of ten, and two sets of pawns. A version of the game was found buried with Tutankhamun.

Games have certainly been used for both education and entertainment for centuries. Still popular today, Snakes and Ladders dates from around 200 BC. It originated in India as a game to teach children about morality. Players progress upwards by climbing ladders (which represent good) and tumble downwards by sliding down snakes (which represent evil).

The most prestigious sports event in the world, the Olympic Games, have been held for centuries and the modern Games still brings millions of people together from across the globe every four years.

We know too that games have such influence on society that governments have frequently banned them. For example, in England, the Unlawful Games Act of 1541, was a comprehensive act passed to proscribe popular games. It was designed to prohibit: 'Several new devised games' that caused 'the decay of archery.' No artisan, husbandman (a small farmer lower in status than a yeoman), labourer, fisherman, waterman or servingman was permitted to play tennis, bowls, quoits, dice, skittles or other 'unlawful' games, except at Christmas.

The act was subsequently repealed of course. The number of public records mentioning breaches of the act suggests that even, under threat of criminal sanctions, the powers that be could not stop people playing games.

It's just a game?

Games give purpose, ritual, meaning, excitement, belonging, combat without killing, dangerous experiences without dying, skill building and more. Games, like stories, are often totally undervalued and misunderstood when people say 'it's just a game'.

When countries qualify for the football World Cup their heads of state have been known to declare a national holiday. During the Cold War, sport became a win-at-all-costs enterprise because it represented a contest between two ideals.

The old adage that football is just 22 people running around kicking a bag of air is actually way off the mark: that's precisely what they are not doing, that's just what it looks like. The Duke of Wellington famously said: 'The battle of Waterloo was won on the playing fields of Eton.' Games teach resilience, pain tolerance, mental toughness, discipline, dedication, commitment, teamwork, personal dignity and tribal affiliation, amongst other things.

The ancient Olympic Games and other ritual games were held to please the gods. Even now, if you watch Usain Bolt and other sporting heroes they often look up to the heavens before the race. Yuzuru Hanyu, the world's greatest ever figure skater goes through incredibly complex rituals before each competition. When Andy Murray won at Wimbledon he looked up to the sky and wagged his finger – a private moment, but he wasn't having a dialogue with anyone on earth that is for sure.

Digital games

Games continue to be an integral part of our lives. Whether we take part in physical sports, watch TV game shows, play card games, word games, solve puzzles or participate in gambling. Games bring us together, help us learn and make life fun.

They are becoming one of the primary mechanisms by which we engage with content and with each other online. Over 2 billion of us are regular game players of one sort or another, evenly split between men and women.

Thomas T. Goldsmith Jr invented the first electronic game back in 1947. The game was described as a 'cathode ray tube amusement device.' Inspired by radar displays from World War II the player used a CRT electron gun to train a beam on a single point on the screen. The dot represented a missile. The player would adjust the dot to hit paper targets fixed to the screen, with all hits detected mechanically. At the time, the first computers were only just being born. Imagine what Mr. Goldsmith could have done with a PlayStation or an Xbox.

In many ways games have come to dominate our culture. The global gaming market today generates more revenue than film and music combined. The early days of Atari's Space Invaders, Asteroids and Pac-Man paved the way for this global phenomenon. Nintendo developed consoles that took electronic games into the home. Smartphones have provided the latest platform for pervasive gaming. In July 2016, Nintendo launched Pokémon Go, an augmented reality game that connected players' real-world surroundings with their digital devices. It quickly became the most downloaded game of all time. It was estimated that global usage peaked at 380 million players only a month after launch – that's one in every twenty people on the planet. Today, virtual reality draws us even deeper into the world of games and is set to launch a new wave of growth in digital gaming.

Why do we play games?

Even if we are not playing games directly, many of us regularly experience them, whether we are learning a new language, pushing for a goal on a fitness app or earning frequent flyers rewards. Many successful tools that engage us and help us to learn do so through our love of games, target setting and competition.

The British psychologist, Donald Winnicott, believed that play is the basis for our creativity and for discovering the self. He described how games create a psychologically safe space to explore and have fun, as well as revealing our internal representations of the world ('Play creates new and fresh meanings', Donald Winnicott, *Playing and Reality*, 1970).

Games are powerful mechanisms for engaging people as they explore stories, experience new concepts and test ideas. Many games these days combine several formats into one to realize different objectives simultaneously. They might be designed to provide the player with many different experiences such as achievement, pleasure, curiosity or challenge. Almost any type of content can be gamified to provide a richer and more interesting experience of the topic.

Play can reinforce some of our most crucial social and life skills – how to play fairly, how to compete, how to win and how to lose. Research has shown that 'games promote deep memory and higher retention among learners' according to Dr Ib Holm Sørensen (2007). Deep or semantic memory is our vital ability to record and recall facts, meanings, concepts and knowledge about our external world, such as gravity, which types of food we like and remembering to say 'thank you.'

It is no coincidence that as we seek to make sense of the new digital world and understand its potential, we are creating more and more games to do so. The fastest growing aspect of game playing is the emergence of massively networked, collaborative games that allow people all over the world to connect with new friends and play together in competitive teams. The first online digital Olympics are due for launch in 2018.

Gamification

Life without games wouldn't resemble life as we know it. Play and games are essential to being human.

Gamification is very much a buzzword today. Gamification is the process of using elements of game-design and game principles to improve the way content engages and motivates people. It typically improves engagement by making content more visual and explorative. It motivates by providing instant feedback on activities, creates community and rewards desired behaviors and results. Store loyalty cards or air miles programmes are simple examples of gamification.

Gamification also transforms educational content into fun, motivating learning that creates an engaging and entertaining experience. Whether it's enhanced reality, simulation, role-playing or a board game, games enable us to explore and learn on our own terms.

Gamification in the digital world is neither a gimmick that technology makes possible nor a kind of luxury that has crossed over from the advances in the gaming world. It's the 21st century version of how we have always learned. It's one of the ways that we have always created satisfying moments and meaning, and one of the ways that we connect with our enthusiasm and feel totally engaged. If you want to see an instance of complete engagement, then ask a teenager to stop playing their PlayStation, even after hours of immersion.

In the past, there has been a prejudicial belief that games and play are the opposite of work and productivity. A better question might be: 'Why is gamification used so little in work and business?' It clearly delivers on so many of the aspects that preoccupy organizations: it engages, motivates and teaches. It offers an experiential element that is far more impactful than textbook learning.

Organizations are realizing that playing games is more than a pastime. They can have significant business results. In fact, some organizations use gaming to differentiate in the market. The original Nike FuelBand was a wearable fitness tracker that kicked off a multi-billion-dollar industry. Customers would track the amount of NikeFuel they used through exercise and daily activity. They competed against other users around the world to see who had the highest score. After reaching a certain level, special prizes and rewards were unlocked. It was highly motivating for Nike's customers, not only to keep doing sports, but also to share their results on social media with a corresponding increase in the brand's visibility. Even as other wearables have taken prominence, NikeFuel remains available as an app on most platforms. With it, Nike gamified the entire fitness industry and reinforced its position as the world's most valuable sportswear brand.

Organizations at play

The application of gamification in learning and engagement has been the subject of many research studies. Johan Huizinga wrote a groundbreaking study on play in 1955 called *Homo ludens: a study of the play element in culture*. He observed that an activity needs to be fully absorbing, include elements of uncertainty and surprise, and involve a sense of illusion or exaggeration. In *Play*, the universe and everything, published in 2005, Tina Bruce gave more definition to play's distinctive qualities:

- It is an active process, intrinsically motivated.

- It is about possible, alternative worlds, which lift players to their highest levels of functioning, making them imaginative, creative, original and innovative.

- It involves reflecting on and becoming aware of what we know (metacognition).

- It actively uses previous first-hand experiences, including struggle, manipulation, exploration, discovery and practice.

- It gets us to use technical prowess, mastery and competence.

- It can be easily initiated by anyone.

- It can be solitary, in partnership or in groups.

- It is an integrating mechanism that brings together everything we learn, know, feel and understand.

Today's digital humans almost certainly have grown up with gaming and are predisposed to the idea of games in the workplace. Even if that's not the case, they are likely to be experiencing – and embracing – the gamification of their everyday lives on an unprecedented scale.

There is a famous social experiment in India, where a set of terminals was placed in a locked building in the centre of a village. The terminals had a networked game on them and the building was opened for one hour every afternoon. Without any instruction at all, local village children figured out how to play the game and within three weeks had not only hacked the locked building but also hacked the system, sending messages to the team behind the game, whom they had never met.

Games and gamification are being taken so seriously that the University of Cambridge has recently appointed its own professor in the subject.

Organizations can build games that define, simulate and test new ideas and concepts. For example, we created a strategy card game for an organization that wanted to entirely redefine its relationship with their customers. The card game enabled the members of the organization to simulate the new customer experience and to understand how they would be required to change their way of doing things to support this new experience. In addition, once they had iterated the card game sufficiently, they were able to test the ideas with customer representatives and then to roll it out to the larger organizational network in order to train everybody.

This process of development and simulation not only forced the team to define the specifics of the change they wanted in quantifiable ways, but it was also done in such a way that change was not perceived as stress. The collaborative development process ensured that many stakeholders were involved in the game. By the time the changes to the customer experience were made formal, almost everyone in the organization had a taste of what was coming. The game reinforced the values of the organization, achieving a series of different benefits through this simple task.

Making games

A simple but useful approach for analyzing and designing games is known as MDA (mechanics, dynamics and aesthetics). It was developed and taught by Robin Hunicke, Marc LeBlanc and Robert Zubek as part of the Game Design and Tuning Workshop at the Game Developers Conference in San Jose (2001–04).

The mechanics are the components of the game: the pieces, the materials, and the prizes. The dynamics describe the run-time behaviours of the game: the impact on the mechanics following a particular input or set of actions. They are essentially the rules that govern the relationships between the elements of the game. The aesthetics describe the players' emotional responses and their thematic, narrative or sensory experience when interacting with the game.

To see these three components at work, let's take golf as an example. In terms of aesthetics, golf is a sensory game, a challenge game as well as one of discovery, particularly if the player has not played a particular golf course before. The run-time dynamics of golf are simple: players take turns to hit their own golf ball from a defined starting position (usually the tee box) with the ultimate goal of sinking it into a hole cut into a green, using only the golf clubs in their bag, in the fewest shots possible. The mechanics of golf include balls, clubs, tees, sand bunkers and water hazards. The combination of weather, nature, and different types of clubs and grass provide for endless variability and challenge, giving many a lifetime of fun and frustration.

As with any design process, we have found it is best to start first with the user experience we intend to create, working backwards from the aesthetics, through dynamics and finishing with the underlying mechanics. Let's take a look at each of these aspects in turn.

Aesthetics

The aesthetics are what make a game interesting and enjoyable to play. The game designer should start first with the type of experience they want to create. Within the MDA approach there are eight defined types of aesthetics:

- Sensation (game as sense pleasure) where the player experiences something completely unfamiliar or a game as an art object that looks, feels or sounds beautiful.

- Fantasy (game as make believe) where the game is set in an imaginary world.

- Narrative (game as drama) where the game is designed around a story that unfolds over time to encourage players to keep coming back.

- Challenge (game as obstacle course) where players are challenged to master something, to solve problems or to make plans.

- Fellowship (game as social framework) where the game emphasizes social interaction, such as multi-player games in which the player takes an active part in a virtual community.

- Discovery (game as uncharted territory) where the player is required to explore a game world.

- Expression (game as self-discovery) where the game encourages the player's own creativity. For example, drawing games or charades.

- Submission (game as pastime) where the game describes the pleasure of a game as a hobby such as knitting or simply organizing books on a shelf.

Most games contain several of these aesthetics. All are fun in their own way. When assessing the purpose and impact of the game, as designers, we can use the terms above to determine what type of fun we intend to provide and why.

Dynamics

Dynamics describes how the governing rules define how a game plays out over time. In the real world, gravity is a dynamic rule. If we drop something, it will fall. In games, for example, dynamics could define how an exchange is made or what happens after a dice is rolled. We could set a competition dynamic by creating a time restriction such as in a car-racing game or a puzzle game. Teamwork dynamics can be encouraged making it easier to solve certain challenges by working with rather than against other players.

The game designers consider how to play and what happens in each particular situation. In good game design, the dynamics should be as simple as possible to understand and use yet create a complex enough experience to be interesting and satisfying. Whenever a game feels like it's too simple or goes on for too long or is too repetitive, it's likely that the game designer has not established the appropriate dynamics.

Mechanics

Mechanics are a combination of the game's content (questions, levels, components and characters) and actions (for example, betting, racing, hitting and shuffling) available to the player.

For example, the mechanics of Monopoly include components, such as houses, hotels, property cards, chance cards, dice, money and counters, and actions such as moving, buying, selling and building. The rules (dynamics) state that each player takes turns to throw the dice, buy property if they can, pay rent or penalties if they need to and win the game by being the last solvent player.

Games require proper and thorough testing with users. We have found that the only way to know if a game actually works is to play it extensively with many different players. Early testing can be conducted with lo-fi mechanics – paper print-outs and simple graphics.

Some of the world's best games are problematic. Take Monopoly once again. As with many games, it has a self-informing feedback system that exaggerates the results of the gameplay – the rich get richer too quickly. The leader or leaders become increasingly wealthy and they can penalize other players with increasing effectiveness. Poorer players become increasingly poor. Dramatic tension is lost, as only one or two players remain invested in the outcome, whilst all other players become disengaged. We know many families that will refuse to play Monopoly for the sake of peace and harmony. When designing games for the people in your organization, pay attention to how the game plays out over time, across a number of different scenarios.

Games in practice

We have been developing applications of games in organizations in many forms to help with the shift to digital. To bring the ideas of this chapter to life, we describe a selection of these games below.

In practice: the business partner cup

One of our clients was looking to encourage their thousands of associates around the world to develop more strategic relationships. They needed these interactions to move beyond simply being transactional.

Because of the international nature of the business, the programme was designed to reinforce learning, collaboration and knowledge in a virtual environment. Through a 3D interactive interface, similar to an online board game, participants took part in a competitive team game. Players could win points for undertaking different actions, such as completing learning activities, posting resources, starting discussions, making comments and even booking sessions in time. A leaderboard showed the overall rankings, as well as rankings by location and business area. Top contributors were rewarded throughout the programme.

The game was designed to be an immersive, state-of-the-art blended learning experience. It used storytelling to create compelling content to ensure the learning material was easy to understand and to apply. As the participants moved through each level, the gameplay and tasks became more intense and complex. Individuals and teams progressed through the game in parallel, completing team challenges and individual activities each week.

Teams of five players competed in cohorts of 300 in a multi-week game. Participation levels were extremely high across the group with an overall completion rate of 92 percent. Analysis of the game showed that it visibly helped to reinforce and embed the knowledge. Participants also enjoyed competing against each other and building relationships across domains during the course of the game. Perhaps most importantly for the business, internal customers' satisfaction of their interactions with business partners increased by 12 percent after the first year of the programme's implementation.

In practice: the margin game

A professional services firm wanted to create an engaging, impactful and motivational game experience for over 10,000 participants that raised awareness about the impact of individual commercial decisions on the wider firm's success, in a playfully competitive way.

A decision (yes/no) game style was designed that provided fictional business and project scenarios with key decisions for players to take. These decisions would have a direct impact on the overall profitability of the project and the business.

Players were required to make decisions to prioritize seemingly conflicting elements, each of which had a different impact on the bottom line. For example, players needed to choose whether to prioritize maintaining an existing client relationship, maximizing revenue, improving project morale or the overall solution quality. Participants advanced through levels of increasing complexity and competed to achieve the highest blended scores. All decisions were tracked, which enabled deep analytics into areas for potential engagement and capability focus. The points system and leaderboards encouraged competition between users.

In practice: gamifying energy security design

An energy company wanted to gamify the process of understanding the impact of policy and strategy decisions on their customer's energy security. The game encoded the key policies, the strategic intent, the elements involved, such as major pipelines and supply routes, as well as the market rules that were in play. This enabled deep investigation of the strategic options and the context in which the decisions could play out.

The game had a series of rounds in which different groups had to compete, negotiate and fight for resources. Scenarios shifted for each of the rounds. The scenarios were adapted from the risk analysis work undertaken by the organization's strategy team. Each of the teams represented the organizations, country or interest groups that were considered the major players. As a result, the organization could experience the various scenarios from the perspective of their competitors, partners or threats. The resulting tactical discussions were far richer than would otherwise have been the case. By playing the game, participants realized major insights and uncovered significant blind spots.

In practice: the drug development process

A pharmaceutical company needed to improve awareness of and participation in the technical research and development of new medicines and the contribution of the research and development function to the wider business.

We created a physical board game and a similar online version that mirrored the process of creating a new medicine from beginning to end. Players drew knowledge cards and collected chips to pass through checkpoints along the journey. We used 3D printing techniques to create bespoke components and playing pieces for each participant, to give the game a unique visual look and feel. The game could be played individually or in teams and was used by thousands of participants across the organization.

The effect of the game was not only to raise awareness of the research and development function, but also to educate the organization about many of the key findings, innovations and programmes. This had a huge impact on the dissemination of new thinking in the organization, leading directly to an increase in innovation across the group.

Next generation gaming

Our involvement and experience with games is going to intensify, as virtual reality becomes widely available, particularly once the new mobile standard, 5G, brings ultra-high definition within reach of everyone everywhere.

These next generation tools are already making a difference to the lives of digital humans, young and old. A patient can track their rehabilitation from a stroke whilst exercising at home through the use of haptic wearables. The more the patient regains sensation, the higher the score on the dashboard. The system encourages the patient to progress further each time. The patient's carer or doctor can track this progress remotely.

The effects of such innovations are being widely felt. Virtual reality is transforming the medical industry. New advances allow trainee surgeons not only to see what is happening in the operating theatre through immersive simulation, but they can feel it as well.

These techniques have broad application – from providing an immersive product demonstration to exploring and testing new services.

As well as games themselves, whether virtual or real, the techniques that lie behind them are being used to make learning experiences less abstract, giving them more context and clearer goals. Through this process of gamification, we are interacting with content in a way that is more playful and immersive.

It's all in the game

Playing games can significantly power up learning and engagement to activate organizations. The mechanics within games can be applied to the content of a wide range of business challenges. It can reinforce and scale up learning. It can encourage more engagement. It can be used to solve problems and generate new ideas. It can support the development of new behaviours. With gamification, organizations can breathe new life into teams.

The process of gamification addresses users as players, putting them at the centre of any experience and creating the architecture of a game around them. Instead of supplying content to be consumed, it provides a competitive experience in which everyone can take part and contribute. Instead of participating in abstract learning, digital humans can operate within a clear context with a defined set of goals. They learn by doing and are encouraged to experiment. Because it is fun, involvement is largely voluntary and self-driven.

Points and rewards are given for different forms of activity, giving individuals and teams instant and constructive feedback. Through this process of playing, we can scaffold learning with more complex tasks, compete on a leaderboard and aspire to become experts. These experts become known within the playing community and can be easily connected to share their know-how.

For digital humans, gamification allows them to take control of their own learning, track their progress and gain satisfaction from performing well. For groups, everyone can operate within a community and build new relationships, as notifications are posted on activities, updates and leaderboards.

Conclusion

Fun, games and competition are at the heart of the next generation of learning and engagement. They have application in gamifying systems by creating simple and engaging ways to share complex ideas, business models and insights. Games can be individual or can promote competition between teams. Gamifying the learning experience enables the learner to test ideas in safe scenarios. Programmes are designed to reward participation and contribution within an engaging environment.

As staunch advocates of bringing play into the workplace, we have found that the gamification of learning materials can be an incredibly powerful way of engaging people and providing them with more rewarding and effective learning experiences. These methods are now overturning the traditional, passive, paper-based ways of informing people. Our love of games and game playing will increasingly impact how we teach, inform and inspire in the digital world.

11.

THE POWER OF SMALL THINGS

'Dripping water hollows out stone, not through force but through persistence.'

Ovid

This chapter is about how to lead change in a digital world. It describes how to shift large complex organizations with light touches. We introduce a set of 'small things' that we have found particularly effective in shifting large organizations. We also explore how to implement such an approach in a sustainable way.

From a single stone

Go is one of the oldest games still played in the world today. Invented in Asia and played in China, Korea and Japan, Go's enduring popularity possibly derives from the simplicity of its rules. Starting with an empty board, each player takes turns to place a piece (called a stone) on the board. One player has a set of white stones, the other a set of black. It is a game of strategy, with the aim being to dominate the board by surrounding and taking your opponent's pieces. Essentially it is about gaining as much territory as possible. Although the rules are very simple, Go is famous for being one of the most complex games in the world. Shen Kuo, an 11th century Chinese scholar, estimated that the number of legal board positions is around 2×10^{172} (he was right). As a comparison, the number of atoms in the observable universe is estimated to be 10^{80}. As Confucius said that people: 'should not waste their time on trivial games - they should study Go.'

Even Go has experienced the power of digital. For many years Go was one of the last places of refuge in which humans could still outperform machines in processing power. It was back in 1997 that IBM's computer Deep Blue beat grandmaster Garry Kasparov in a chess match and made news around the world. However, it wasn't until October 2015, that a computer programme called AlphaGo beat world-class human professional Go player, Lee Sedol. Following this, in 2017, AlphaGo beat Ke Jie, the world No1 ranked player at the time, in a three-game match. After the match, Ke Jie said: 'After humanity spent thousands of years improving our tactics, computers tell us that humans are completely wrong ... I would go as far as to say not a single human has touched the edge of the truth of Go.' AlphaGo was able to win by playing moves and deploying strategies that a human player would never have conceived, because it has seen moves that no human ever has.

AlphaGo demonstrates the ability of software and computing power to understand and influence complex systems. This way of thinking and understanding, vital to leading digital organizations, will enable us to use a myriad of small things to nudge our organizations towards greater excellence, efficiency, employee and customer satisfaction or whatever the desired strategic outcome we aspire to.

Go is fascinating because players need to influence a highly dynamic environment and do so with the lightest of touches. A strong player needs to be able to read far ahead into the game. Some of the best players can read up to 40 moves ahead even in complex situations. For every move, they need to find the greatest impact possible by playing a single piece. When the conditions are right, one particularly good move can impact almost every piece on the board, turning the entire game. Like Go, digital organizations are highly dynamic environments that can be influenced by the smallest of things.

The shift from mechanistic, rules-based organizations to digital ecosystems requires a shift in leadership approach. How do we influence, direct and shift organizations to stay relevant and be successful? How do we find the greatest points of leverage? How can digital tools help us orchestrate change across our new tribal teams?

Call me trim tab

During World War I, Anton Flettner developed what is now the 'trim tab' that is still widely in use on all airplanes and many large ships. The trim tab is a small hinged strip of metal attached to rudders and wings that allows them to be moved while under great force. As an engine's hydraulics move the trim tab into the path of oncoming water or air, the pressure generated assists in making a turn. The key to getting the best results from the trim tabs is to operate them in short half-second bursts and then letting the boat or plane react before making another adjustment.

By nudging the aircraft or vessel as it 'trims' along its journey, trim tabs are an example of small things in the right place that help to make the big change in overall direction. Trim tabs were much loved by Buckminster Fuller, the visionary American inventor and designer, who said:

> Something hit me very hard once, thinking about what one little man could do. Think of the Queen Mary — the whole ship goes by and then comes the rudder. And there's a tiny thing at the edge of the rudder called a trim tab.
>
> It's a miniature rudder. Just moving the little trim tab builds a low pressure that pulls the rudder around. Takes almost no effort at all. So I said that the little individual can be a trim tab. Society thinks it's going right by you, that it's left you altogether. But if you're doing dynamic things mentally, the fact is that you can just put your foot out like that and the whole big ship of state is going to go.
>
> So I said, call me trim tab.

Trim tabs are vital in transforming complex organizations. They are shorthand for reminding us to apply the minimum effort for the maximum impact to stay on course. Consider oil tankers too large for the Suez Canal. They have to pass the Cape of Good Hope and make huge turns in some of the roughest waters as they round the tip of Africa. A large tanker cannot be turned by brute force alone; it needs to be nudged into a new direction through small and continuous adjustments to its six-storey-high rudder.

Nudge, nudge

Much of the effort involved in organizational change is directed at encouraging people to adopt new ways of working. In this regard, there is a strategic imperative for enabling individuals or small teams to create impactful results with better thinking and tools in less time. What are the trim tabs to consider when leading digital humans?

A nudge is defined as a light touch or push. As we mentioned in our chapter on trends, nudge theory was named and popularized by the 2008 book, *Nudge: improving decisions about health, wealth, and happiness*, written by the American academics, Richard H Thaler and Cass R Sunstein. The book draws on the Nobel prize-winning work of the psychologists Daniel Kahneman and Amos Tversky.

Nudge theory is based on indirect encouragement and enablement. It avoids direct instruction or enforcement. For example, to lose weight, a brute force method might be to restrict calorie intake or ban certain foods. A nudge would simply involve the use of a smaller plate.

Advertisers have long known that we humans can be nudged to consume more of a particular product. There is, of course, the story of the clever marketer who doubled sales of a shampoo product by adding the final word to the instructions: 'Lather. Rinse. Repeat.' In the 1960s, the agency Tinker & Partners created 'a frothy, luminous commercial composed of nothing but two Alka-Seltzers dropping into a crystal glass of water'. Following a meeting with a lab doctor who confirmed that taking two Alka-Seltzers would be better than one in easing pain, their advertisement was designed with the phrase: 'Two Alka-Seltzers'.

Prior to this, both the commercials and packaging of Alka-Seltzer had directed the use of only a single tablet at a time. Alka-Seltzer sales didn't quite double, but the company certainly experienced a complete reversal of fortune due to the Tinker & Partners commercials. The suggestion for consumers to take two tablets — later reinforced with the enduring 'plop, plop; fizz fizz' jingle – dispelled the notion previously established in the minds of the public that anyone should ever take fewer than two Alka-Seltzers at a time.

The public and health sectors have recently embraced the idea of nudging with great gusto. One of the earliest adopters was the UK's Cabinet Office, whose behavioural insights team (dubbed the 'nudge unit') blazed a trail in nudging people towards a whole range of good behaviours by making subtle changes to the way the government communicated its services and policies.

One of its greatest successes saw a significant rise in income tax payments after a reminder letter was simply reworded to say that 'most people in your neighbourhood have already paid their tax'. That particular insight understood that most of us are uncomfortable about flouting social norms and that our behavior is profoundly influenced by what others are seen to be doing.

Nudges are powerful. In an interview with the New York Times, Richard Thaler said that whenever he is asked to autograph a copy of Nudge, he signs it: 'Nudge for good'. With the possibility to create powerful and lasting change, today's leaders should keep the same principle in mind when nudging the people they work with to adopt new behaviours.

Nudges can have a clear effect in corralling and shifting very large groups without using command and control. They are typically inexpensive and easy to implement. The challenge is to find ones that will influence behaviour in a way that becomes self-sustaining. When such nudges go viral, the effect can be dramatic. As in the game of Go, one nudge shifts the entire organization. One of the key shifts for leaders is to understand that in the digital domain, their role has also significantly changed.

The digital leader

'There are two things I go back to again and again: having the right people and working on the right problem.'

Caterina Fake

Leading a digital organization requires a different set of skills and behaviours. The playing field has changed and new rules are in place. At present, many leaders believe that they sit at the top of hierarchies that do their bidding. Within the digital realm they are simply a single node in a vast digital web of connections.

Many leaders today are still playing chess when in fact they need to be playing Go. In the past, a leader needed to have a clear vision and the personal firepower to make it happen. Today's leaders need a new set of skills. They need to be media-savvy, technology-savvy as well as digital business-savvy. They are managing a shifting ecosystem and need to be able to demonstrate clear leadership even as the business continually changes around them.

We have worked with so many organizations where employees say they 'aren't clear on the strategy'. The reason for this is not because there isn't a strategy; rather, it's because the strategy changes so quickly that traditional ways of communicating it are ineffective. Messages from the top are easily lost amid the cacophony of mass communication. By the time the strategy can be implemented the situation has already moved on. Digital leaders need to be able to command attention in new ways. We need to stay ahead of the narrative, by being able to use social media with the same impact as we assess a profit-and-loss statement.

One example of a leader who got everyone's attention and won by changing the game is Alexander the Great. From a small state in northern Greece he conquered the known world and overthrew 3000 years of imperial Persian history. We tend to focus on the military drama that accompanied his reign. It is just as captivating to consider how he had such a grand and lasting influence on civilization that he came to be called 'the Great.'

In 15 years of war, Alexander never lost a battle. Considered one of the greatest military geniuses in history, he was a supreme tactician able to adapt his approach depending on such factors as the nature of the enemy or type of terrain. He created a more agile force that could be quickly re-located and manoeuvered. He transformed his soldiers' weapons, arming them with short stabbing spears and giving them light armour. By changing the direction of attack, he confused the opposing armies who were trained to meet head on. One note for armchair commanders: Alexander always led from the front, clearly visible to his troops in every battle.

In order to sustain his new world, Alexander relied on a series of cultural shifts to bring about permanent changes in the societies he conquered. He founded cities, often named after himself. He imposed his own legal system. He accepted and co-opted local gods, usually making himself one of them. He encouraged his generals to marry locally. It was a system of law and civilization that proved so compelling that many of Alexander's enemies chose to surrender rather than resist, thereby creating a cultural legacy we still have today.

We think Alexander has some great lessons for digital leaders today.

- He constantly surrounded himself with experts from the local people in his new lands. The greatest legacy his father gave him was his education. He learned from Aristotle the power of working with local experts.

- He worked to understand the new cultures that came into his empire and honoured their most important ideals, whilst simultaneously transforming them.

- He knew how to organize and motivate a mobile, fast-moving force. Every soldier had simple rules to follow, depending on their role.

- He wasn't afraid to try radical new solutions. Remember the Gordian Knot, a rope with an unbreakable knot at the palace of Gordium? The legend had it that whoever could 'loose the knot' would be the ruler of all Asia. Alexander drew his sword and cut the knot in two demonstrating how he did not accept conventional ways of doing things and tapping into local mythology to promote his personal power narrative.

Using the power of small things

From our experience we recommend focusing on four specific ways a digital leader can use the power of small things to enable an organization to self-transform. These are: simplifiers, timers, connectors and attractors.

Simplifiers

Simplifiers make it easy for people to behave in ways that achieve the desired result by making use of prompted choices and defaults, removing friction or obstacles and presenting key messages clearly and simply. For example, a workspace could be reconfigured to allow teams to interact more easily and encourage collaboration. Other examples of simplifiers could be reducing the number of available buying options for a customer or pre-filling certain boxes on a form by default.

Simplifiers make it more likely that an individual will make a certain choice.

Timers

Timers create a specific moment or time window in which it would be best to act. For example, booking a holiday early to secure a discount or having a makeover in preparation for an important birthday or event.

Timers can be implemented at key moments during the transformation programme. Well-timed messages and prompts make a great difference to understanding and engagement during periods of transition. Providing a countdown to an important event or a daily reminder to complete an activity are helpful timers in shifting behaviour.

Connectors

Connectors are changes in behaviour that result from what other people do. Just as tribes tend to adopt similar clothes, mannerisms and mindsets, individuals connected to others share what they are doing and are more likely to take the same or similar actions.

The take-up of a new initiative can be increased by working with people positioned locally across the organization to champion and highlight the benefits of the new initiative. Alternatively, we can harness the power of social networks to encourage colleagues to make visible commitments to others about the actions they intend to take and work they are focusing on. Connections through forums, discussion groups and challenges amplify these ideas throughout the system. Encouraging groups to form around specific ideas, to engage, knowledge share and learn from experts is highly likely to create the conditions for a shift in understanding and behavior.

Attractors

Attractors are designed to grab attention and make a particular course of action appealing or salient. These are often most compelling when personalized and make use of games and incentives to motivate people to engage.

A striking example of the power of attractors comes from Coca-Cola, whose famous 'Share a Coke' campaign saw millions around the world seek out their own names on personalized bottles. Other ways to use attractors include competitions and awards that recognize particular types of behaviour or action.

In the chapter 'Build beautiful things', we highlighted the importance of considering the aesthetic form when developing solutions and communicating ideas. By making things attractive to others, expressing benefits in a visually clear and tangible way, we will draw people towards not away from new thinking.

The impact of building representations of the new ideas, such as collaboratively authoring new games, or defining the storyboards for video media and websites together, cannot be underestimated. For example, the collaborative authoring of a new media campaign by a large number of stakeholders is in itself a powerful nudge for the entire organization to embrace its new identity.

Sustaining momentum

Nudges and trim tabs are the mechanics of large-scale change. As with designing games, we have to put in place the dynamics for them to work and to make changes in real time. No change happens in a straight line except in a vacuum. Every shift from one state to the next relies on a series of turns and corrections. A boat tacks through the water. A plane triangulates towards its destination. How can we implement these methods to unleash massive change in a controlled and manageable way?

Consider how skiers safely descend a mountain. They do so through a series of turns. For a skier to execute each turn, they typically use three techniques: establishing a pivot point; using gravity to make the turn; and then rebalancing to properly exit the turn and maintain consistent momentum. The language of slalom skiing is useful for leaders.

Finding the pivot point

As any ski instructor will advise, it is important to plant the ski pole in front and to the side, so as to turn safely around it. The pole becomes a pivot that acts as the centre of gravity. In the same way, when aiming to change direction, a leader should find a solid centre point, a guiding principle for example, that will not be directly affected by the change. This pivot point gives stability and order as everything else turns around it. The pivot point could be maintaining the customer experience, for instance, whilst introducing a new technology system. Alternatively, it could be a set of company values that describe the priorities to remain constant for the organization, even as the day-to-day business changes course.

Making the turn

Just as skiers constantly make small adjustments to their balance and technique as they turn down the mountain, so organizations need to experiment and fine-tune the way they nudge and trim tab through change. We have found that often small changes in language have big implications. For example, we encourage our teams not to apologize for mistakes, but to describe what they intend to do differently or better in the future. We try not to talk about issues, but rather talk about challenges. Issues go on a list — challenges have to be overcome.

We also promote the role of 'community animators' who can sequence an appropriate set of nudges throughout a programme to continuously keep the work and the teams focused. Staying on track is particularly important and requires attention when working virtually. Community animators foster a sense of collective purpose and give practical support through coaching, notifications and reminders. They help teams to learn and share by starting discussions, highlighting milestones and posting resources.

Maintaining momentum

Having learned the basics, the biggest problem novice skiers experience is controlling their speed. This is normally because they do not fully complete each turn before entering the next. This causes them to speed up and lose control.

It is the same in organizations. Each major change needs to be properly completed prior to starting a new intervention. Otherwise the organization can slip into stasis or chaos with too many moving and unconnected parts. For large programmes, the community animators are instrumental. They help maintain a steady drum beat of momentum. They ensure focus and motivation when change becomes too complex and activate greater connectivity between individuals if the work becomes stuck.

In the chapter 'Turn it on', we explore how to build and maintain momentum in more depth.

In practice: breakthrough leaders

In the years following the financial crash of 2008, the perception and the culture of many financial institutions can best be described as toxic. We were invited to work with a financial services organization that needed to completely shift the culture within their organization as well as make significant changes to how they carried out business.

We developed a programme called Breakthrough Leaders that was initially for the most senior leaders. These top 100 leaders participated in a series of immersive learning events and masterclasses that took place both physically and online. During these sessions, the leaders connected to some of the best people in the world on customer service, leadership, entrepreneurship, innovation, technology and values.

They worked with these experts alongside our production teams to create films and multi-media toolkits that synthesized their learnings, key messages and the practices with which they wanted to influence their organization.

There was then an online campaign across the organization. Leaders used these multi-media toolkits with their teams to introduce new ways of working and nudge behaviours. The HR director responsible at the time said: 'The Breakthrough Leaders programme was designed with only one goal in mind: to help our leaders become the best they could be, by working together to redefine our industry and lead our business through these difficult times and into a strong competitive position as the new market landscape took shape.'

Conclusion

There are too many competing elements to ever move in a straight line when seeking to implement change. In the physical world there are forces such as gravity, wind, friction and tides. For organizations, they experience forces in the same way, as priorities, economics, technologies and markets constantly change.

Alexander the Great made relatively small but significant changes in his 33 years that have impacted the world for millennia and his name will never be forgotten.

For leaders pursuing systemic change, it can seem surprising that a series of small, relatively inexpensive adjustments can have such a dramatic effect. Behavioural scientists, however, have established that we respond best to indirect encouragement and enablement.

In this way, command or control is not required. Through the power of small things, leaders establish the conditions for organizations to navigate their own way through digital disruptions and start transforming outcomes.

SECTION 4:

LEARNING AND GETTING TO THE NEXT LEVEL

12.

TARGETS AND THE MIRROR

'Mirror, mirror, on the wall,
Who in this land is fairest of all?'

From *Snow White*
by Jacob and Wilhelm Grimm

Within digital organizations, an immense amount of feedback is available. How well we incorporate all this input impacts our performance. For leaders, the mapping of this landscape of reflected data is now becoming one of the primary tasks in navigating a changing world.

The great civilizer

We have had mirrors for almost as long as people have walked the earth. So the story goes, the first mirror was formed when the waters of a small stream in the Himalayas paused as if considering which way to turn and while the waters were still, reflected the image of a passing girl who had herself paused to glance into the stream.

Perhaps the best-known story of fascination with our own reflection is the Greek myth of Narcissus; the beautiful hunter so fascinated by the face he sees in a pool that he cannot pull himself away. Unlike his Himalayan counterpart, he fails to realize it's his own reflection he has fallen in love with, and so pines away on the riverbank.

Even Socrates had something to say on the usefulness of seeing our reflection. We are told by Diogenes that he recommended young people should 'look at themselves in mirrors so that, if they were beautiful, they would become worthy of their beauty, and if they were ugly, they would know how to hide their disgrace through learning'. That might sound a little harsh or unsavoury to our modern ear, but the subtext is that we should avoid pride by knowing our limits, whilst always seeking to improve ourselves. In this sense, Socrates saw the mirror as a tool by which to 'know thyself'.

We have always been fascinated by seeing our own reflection and this has more than a little to do with our need for feedback: Does our internal sense of identity match our external appearance? What can we divine from our own reflection that gives us clues about who and what we are? As in the case of Narcissus, this feedback if not properly understood can be dangerous: Narcissus is a useful reminder to examine our perceptions and a warning against the prison of self-absorption. If we take Socrates' position, our reflection can be the feedback mechanism by which to know ourselves better.

Looking inside

'Dou miroir par double maniere
Pues tu veoir oevre pleniere'
['Gentle mirror in two ways
You can fully expose everything']

Jean de Condé,
Le dis dou miroir

In *Le dis dou miroir* by Jean de Condé, a man requests a double mirror, to look at himself 'inside and out.' He wrote: 'A mirror must be present day and night, a mirror whose obverse is obscure and diverse.'

Shakespeare's *Hamlet* explained to his actors that the 'purpose of playing' is 'to hold as 'twere the mirror up to nature, to show virtue her feature, scorn her own image, and the very age and body of the time his form and pressure'. In other words, he implores them to create something so real that they can see themselves and their own world within the roles they present on the stage. The players in Shakespeare's Hamlet, intend to create a play so real that it becomes real.

Organizations also know that feedback is essential to growth and success. Feedback informs how well we are performing and what we need to adjust both from an external and internal perspective. To understand how to give and take feedback to educate ourselves and others, is a vital skill in being successful. Simply holding up the mirror isn't the answer. Too much feedback at one time can paralyze the system, just as Narcissus was paralyzed by his own image. Digital tools provide more than just a mirror. They can shine a light on the very inner workings of an organization and even show us the path ahead.

Digital mirrors

We live in a world of signals. Some signals are like beacons along the coastline: scattered, not complete, but collectively describing the shape of the land. Some are weak signals: things that exist now that will scale to dominate in the future.

A digitally connected organization essentially has a nervous system. It can gather feedback from any point. The information available is only limited by the number and position of sensors in the system. Any connected technology from a single security turnstile to a fully automated production line provides data that can inform decision-making.

For organizations, feedback from such sensors is now available through so many channels, devices and formats that it is difficult to know what to focus on and when. Every individual, often without knowing it, is continually capturing and providing feedback through their digital devices.

Algorithms that geo-locate us through our smartphones provide real-time data to traffic and transport systems, which in return recommend the quickest route. Systems that track our online searches and shopping determine future advertisements and make recommendations for further purchases. Retailers are able to dynamically change their pricing depending on stock volumes and demand on an hourly basis.

Off the windswept west coast of South Africa, out in the South Atlantic, fishermen are using mobile phone apps to better understand where to fish and to catch only as many fish as the market requires. It also means they can sell their catch before they even reach the shore.

For digital humans and organizations alike, being able to navigate the volume of data and feedback available is a complex task. When used well, it can lead to better decision-making and outcomes. What are the appropriate sensors for your organization and how much connectivity is required to navigate?

The right amount of connectivity

In a breakthrough in evolutionary thinking in the early 1990s, championed by Stuart Kaufmann, a biologist at the Santa Fe Institute, it was suggested that there are better explanations for how life began than the random mechanism of Darwin's natural selection. The team came to the conclusion that a collection of inanimate molecules could together create enough complexity to start a chain of chemical and biological reactions with the appropriate level of connectivity to form life.

They described how systems always exist in two principal states – order and chaos. Between them lies a thin line on the edge of chaos, which creates the most interesting set of future possibilities and from which a new order spontaneously creates itself.

Order is when the system remains constant and unchanging after a period of time. Chaos occurs when all components of the system continuously change their state, even after no further stimulus. There are extremes at each end of the spectrum. A system that is overly connected becomes frozen and cannot change. Too little connectivity leads to random and chaotic behaviour. Imagine a team playing field hockey. If the players are positioned too far apart the ball cannot be passed quickly between them. If they all stand next to each other, the ball cannot be moved. A decent team works together dynamically to stay sufficiently connected to allow the ball to be passed quickly and efficiently.

In his thesis, Kaufmann suggests that a system will be optimally connected when each component is connected with two other components. Sports teams would no doubt agree: they should always have two players available to receive the ball. It's a principle well worth keeping in mind when establishing relationships between different parts of the organization or asking team members to provide feedback about their performance to each other. It's advisable to establish two main points of feedback for each individual.

With the sheer volume of possible data points available, how can an organization make sense of this mass of information to make better decisions and plan ahead?

Making sense of the data

'Where is the Life we have lost in living?
Where is the wisdom we have lost in knowledge?
Where is the knowledge we have lost in information?'

T.S. Eliot

There is a famous model called the data, information, knowledge and wisdom pyramid. It describes a hierarchy of sense-making. Although we find these terms useful, we find it overly simplistic to think of knowledge as a stacked, hierarchical construct. Knowledge is not an aggregate of data and reports. It is developed over time constructively through experience by making things and using them in the real world. For an activated organization, we are interested in ensuring everyone and everything in the system has the appropriate level of information to be able to make useful decisions autonomously. Not just the leaders. This requires frameworks and simple rule sets for people and technology to make sense of the data.

You may have seen a murmuration of starlings flying together. They are never led by a single individual, but instead work together using a very simple set of rules, such as move when your neighbour moves. They act independently but with enough understanding of their companions to form incredibly complex and beautiful formations.

Another example, lean management, based on the Toyota production system, provides a set of simple tools such as A3 thinking,

177

which form a framework for individual decision-making. This ensures that a team or individual focuses only on the information needed to achieve their objective at a particular point in time. Here, the framework acts less like a mirror and more like a magnifying glass.

A connected set of machines can also inform decision-making. For example, Coca-Cola has placed sensors in their vending machines that allow them to collect data on which drinks sell best at what time of day. The sensors detect which machines are busiest and when products are running low. Some even act as a wi-fi hotspot. These intelligent vending machines form part of a connected and more optimized supply chain and inform autonomous procurement decisions. The Internet of Things is creating a web of connected sensors that organizations and individuals tap into as part of their sense-making. Artificial intelligence can provide qualitative recommendations and even make autonomous decisions based on far greater data sets than humans are able to process.

Together this connected field of people and digital technology provides a sufficiently complex and diverse environment in which an organization will evolve.

Making a map

When the first cartographers were making maps of our world they used the terms 'here be dragons' or 'terra incognita' to label an unknown or unexplored land.

Leaders in the digital world need to have a far greater sense of the systemic map of their organizations. They need an understanding of the technology systems, people roles, customer markets and all the other elements that connect and work together.

Rather than direct every aspect, the leaders' role is to bring context and purpose. We need to maintain and make sense of the map and (as we described in the previous chapter) to use the power of small things to nudge the organization towards the goals. The effectiveness of projects and teams can be seen in digital dashboards that provide live information. These dashboards join the dots between different data sources to improve decision-making. They provide interpolation and visualization of highly complex data sets and present patterns that highlight areas of risk or high performance.

For example, leaders no longer need to wait for the annual employee survey to discover the engagement levels of staff – it can be detected on a daily basis through an array of sensors linked directly to specific tasks. Semantic analysis of participation in an online forum discussing a new element of strategy, will reveal which areas of the business are highly engaged and which require further attention. Leaders can then make appropriate interventions in good time.

Navigating into the future

How can organizations navigate the digital future and use feedback to monitor progress towards their objectives? We recommend paying attention to three areas:

Identify the sensors

It's vital to understand what's in the periphery of the organization's vision. Look for the rumours circulating both inside and outside the organization. Capture signals and chatter from customers, competitors, influencers, as well as societal and political changes. What are the essential (and minimal) sensors required to provide feedback on the economic, technical and cultural performance within the organization both from an external and internal perspective?

Connect the data

Digital organizations need to create the conditions to stay on the edge between stasis and chaos with the right flow of feedback to stay alive and evolve. Settling on the most appropriate level of connectivity is how organizations will find the most scope for realizing new possibilities. Connectivity is about promoting the flow of knowledge between people. This is the point where a new order creates itself spontaneously and where teams will be able to act autonomously.

Build the map

Digital enables us to work with far more complex and better quality datasets. It also provides the tools and apps for making sense of them. The digital organization exists within an ever-changing data cloud. Understanding the shapes of this cloud using visual tools and assessing how information shifts relative to the desired outcomes is one of the key skills needed by digital leaders.

Conclusion

As we have learned from Narcissus, it's not helpful to just hold up a mirror and reflect data back. It can be completely overwhelming and destructive. Narcissus fell in love with his own reflection to his detriment.

In the digital organization, the sensory information, in all its forms, is the organization. What is a digital organization? It is the sum total of all the data, information and knowledge that is exchanged. It is the ephemeral shape of the cloud of data that it generates. This data is far more than a mirror. It is its identity.

To take soundings on a regular basis profoundly supports learning. This knowledge enables us to understand our context, it keeps ships off the rocks and it enables the digital organization to safely navigate unchartered waters.

For an organization to evolve, it requires a high variety of diverse ideas. It needs to create opportunities to combine and test them, putting them under selective pressure. Then it needs to implement the best of them. These are the elements that enable digital organizations to be alive.

13.

ALWAYS LEARNING

'Educating the mind without educating the heart is no education at all.'

Aristotle

This chapter is about the future of learning and why digital humans will need to commit to continuous learning as a life skill. We also present how organizations can deliver highly personalized, highly effective learning at a huge scale, using the opportunities presented by digital.

The House of Wisdom

In the 9th and 10th centuries, Baghdad grew to be the largest city worldwide and was at the centre of the golden age of Islam. Its founder, Caliph al-Mansur of the Abbasid, is said to have chosen the location for Baghdad because of its mild climate, secure geography, proximity to the Tigris and its link to the main trade routes of the day. Baghdad became a focal point of culture and learning.

At this time, an incredible library named Khizanat al-Hikma (Library of Wisdom) was created by Caliph Harund Al-Rasheed. The Caliph required somewhere to house the manuscripts and books that had been amassed by his father and grandfather, in many different languages, covering subjects across the arts and sciences. The collection grew so large that his son, Caliph Al-Ma'mun, decided to extend the original building and turn it into an academy. The new building was re-named Bayt al-Hikma (the House of Wisdom) and was home to many different branches of knowledge.

People from all over the world gathered in the House of Wisdom, both male and female, from many faiths and backgrounds. Within its walls, philosophers, scientists, scribes and writers would convene every day to read, write and discuss many and varied topics. The House of Wisdom became a centre for the translation of manuscripts and books covering subjects and ideas from all over the known world.

During the reign of al-Ma'mun, astronomical observatories were created and the House became the foremost centre for learning in the world. On the basis of mainly Greek texts but also texts in Persian, Sanskrit and Syriac, which were translated into Arabic, they accumulated an incredible collection of world knowledge. By the middle of the 9th century, the House of Wisdom held the largest collection of books in the world.

The goal was to spread a new ideology with a political and scientific basis. Baghdad's location on the banks of the Tigris made it ideal for water-powered paper mills, which allowed for the production of paper and books at a lower cost. Ideas were transmitted to many more people through the written word.

The House of Wisdom established a model of learning and knowledge transfer that has echoed around the globe.

A thirst for knowledge

Humans have always had a desire for learning and it is through the gathering of knowledge and education that our species has progressed. From agricultural society through industrial society to the knowledge economy and now digital, each epoch has required its own sets of life skills and knowledge. Shifts in political economy from feudalism to industrialization and with it, democracy, required different knowledge bases for people to perform the different roles in civil society. Democracy doesn't work without an educated populace who are able to critically discern, use facts for decision-making, rhetoric for persuasion and motivate themselves to contribute and vote.

There has been a seismic disruption to our global society. Digital and the impact of Facebook, Twitter and YouTube on the political process are only now in 2018 starting to be understood. The outcomes of the US election and the Brexit vote in the UK in 2016 will perhaps define the point at which social media became a primary channel through which political discourse is conducted. So too, the nature of work is shifting dramatically. Organizations, engulfed as they are by social media and new apps, are faced with continuous disruption from the streams of knowledge and communication that inundate them – social, political, regulatory, technological and economic.

In the face of these pressures, we believe that the skills associated with continuous learning are key for an adaptive, competitive workforce to be able to make sense of it all. Concepts such as critical thinking, synthesis, prototyping and constructivist documentation (how we develop knowledge and create meaning through making things) will become part of our everyday life skills.

For people living longer with potentially multiple or portfolio careers, learning is the fuel that powers interesting and continually relevant lives. Take surgeons, for example. Operations can now be conducted by remote 'tele-surgery' where a patient is operated on by a robot controlled through a virtual-reality system by an experienced surgeon at another location. We doubt they learned that skill 20 years ago in medical school.

Not least because many of the jobs of the future have not yet been invented, we will be continually learning new skills throughout our lives. For the vast majority of people, learning will not end after school or university. We understand more and more what lifelong learning means. For example, we may subscribe to branded sources of knowledge, such as the Open University, The London School of Economics and Political Science, Yale or Harvard Universities, through which we will continually refresh and learn new skills. A university place may become for life. Intelligent learning platforms will make personalized recommendations for our learning and continuously curate for us learning content relevant to our current and future roles. Future employers or teams will be able to verify our CVs from an accredited blockchain powered index.

We no longer have to travel to a house of wisdom or even the local library for our learning. Every one of us has immediate access to our own personal house of wisdom, one infinitely more vast and accessible than the original, any time we need, right in our own hands. The role of universities may shift to include the validation of source materials ensuring we can trust the libraries we subscribe to. The digital world is capable of providing everyone with access to high-quality knowledge anytime, anywhere – if we know where to look.

The future of learning for digital humans is about getting what we want, when we want it and in the way we want it.

Why elearning doesn't work

To achieve results, we need to consider the design, the process, the system, the content and the context. Learning isn't just about technology. One of our favourite examples is compliance training. This can often be elearning at its worst: out-of-date slides and a tedious, narrative-free set of rules to remember. Just like classroom training, virtual learning must take a human-centric approach and be made relevant for people across different generations and from diverse backgrounds. Two great examples we saw recently are the pre-flight safety films on United Airlines and British Airways flights. Certainly, they were more expensive to produce, but they made brilliant use of story, imagery and humour to bring familiar content to life in a new way.

As organizations become more global and more disparate, traditional training methods become impractical. Face-to-face events and workshops are difficult to scale and expensive to run. For many years, elearning has been seen as a viable alternative, being quickly scalable and often cheaper. As we described in our look at trends, even at its best, elearning is typically one-dimensional. Whilst it may suffice when studying a technical, specialized subject, it really is just one mode of learning. In many cases, elearning is little more than a slide deck online – an ineffective way for adults to learn and retain information. For the purposes of our own research, we've asked many people what they think of elearning. The overwhelming answer is clear: they don't like it and they don't engage with it.

Millions of dollars are spent on ineffective learning systems and solutions. We know of several global organizations that have multiple (20+) learning management systems in place and many thousands of online courses that their people cannot easily access or aren't relevant to their work. Many of these learning management systems have become like the local lending libraries of old. A place to store out-of-date books that nobody reads. Yet even the local library has had to re-invent itself. The way that successful local libraries have responded to the changing needs of society has been to re-discover their purpose as a centre of learning and knowledge exchange. Today, the best of them facilitate knowledge transfer through discussion groups, activity centres for learning and more, just like the great libraries of ancient times.

By comparison, learning management systems have simply not kept up. Many are still just a place full of hard-to-find and unuseful content. Many learning managers actively avoid using their own learning systems to deliver learning. Organizations have come to realize that they cannot re-create a model of face-to-face, expert-led classroom training by simply hosting a plethora of unstructured courses in an online library.

Learning expectations

The expectations individuals have for their own learning are also changing. Just as with the media they consume, digital humans seek highly tailored, individual learning experiences. For many people, their experience of learning is easier and more effective outside of work than inside. From a child learning a new trick on their bike to an adult learning to play a new piece of music or construct a piece of furniture, digital humans can find out how to do almost anything with a few seconds of online searching and viewing.

Organizations are dealing with a far more demanding audience. Individuals, who are used to immersing themselves in interactive games and online shows in their personal lives, now have a much higher expectation of the quality of learning content delivery at work.

For individual learners, how they learn is as important as what is being learnt. There has been a massive societal shift. People are used to constructing their own narratives and making their own movies. They will require a future in society and their work in which they experience a similar level of autonomy and control over their choices and their learning.

Digital changes everything

As Peter Senge described in his seminal work, *The Fifth Discipline*, learning organizations build capability quickly and in cost-effective ways that adapts to support their evolving strategy. Senge was certainly ahead of his time and nearly three decades later, many organizations are only now coming to understand the importance of implementing his ideas.

We know from adult learning theory (popularized by Malcolm Shepherd Knowles) that adults are selective in what they choose to learn and that they take responsibility for their own learning. They bring their own life experiences to theory and respond best to problem-solving approaches with peers. The well-known 70:20:10 approach suggests that 70 percent of all learning should be through experience or 'on the job', 20 percent should be through social interaction and feedback from others and just 10 percent should be through structured courses and training.

Therefore, to be successful, the best adult learning programmes will include a blend of techniques including self-learning, collaborative learning, classroom and problem-based learning, experiential and narrative learning, learning communities and action learning teams. The challenge for organizations today is how to provide a high degree of personalization whilst delivering such a rich blend of learning techniques at scale.

Digital resolves many of the issues that traditional learning methods present for organizations seeking to become learning organizations. Digital means that transformational learning (learning that affects us on an identity level and positively effects our beliefs and behaviours) can now be delivered at the required scale.

Digital can provide the curated-learning content and bespoke individual learning pathways that Senge imagined. Digital learning organizations can equip their people with the skills, knowledge and behaviours they need to be successful within their roles and to support the organizational strategy in far faster timescales than previously possible. Learning becomes the organizational modus operandi and not just an adjunct to the work.

Next generation learning

We call this approach to delivering transformational learning through digital 'next generation learning'. It is a completely different learning experience. To bring it to life, here's an example from one of our projects.

In practice: next generation learning for shared services

Our client had created a global centre for shared services and was looking to develop higher level relationships and strategic interactions between stakeholders across the business. Previously, the approach was to hold face-to-face workshops, with 20 people flying in at a time. This was popular but could not be delivered at the scale the organization had set in the time frames required. It was time for innovation.

The challenge was to create a learning experience with the same intensity and impact as the face-to-face programme, but conducted entirely virtually, involving not just a score of people, but hundreds.

Way beyond elearning, the progamme is a complete example of next generation learning that uses the power of digital to create bespoke learning journeys for everybody. It brings together self-learning, virtual classrooms, coaching, team sessions, community interaction and games. It can be delivered whenever and wherever the individual chooses. When participants join the programme, they set up their own profile, identify their preferred learning styles and set their own learning objectives. The system provides every participant with a personalized learning journey through a curriculum tailored to their needs.

Participants choose a business challenge that they are experiencing in their daily activities. This allows them to apply their knowledge to a live issue. Managers help align these challenges with the current priorities of the team. Expert coaches support by stretching learners through one-to-one sessions via video conferences.

Virtual classrooms are provided throughout the programme. Each is scheduled to last for three hours. The virtual classrooms are made available at multiple times and participants select the sessions that suit their own schedule. Learners join the virtual classrooms from anywhere in the world. They collaborate together both as a group and in break-out sessions to dynamically test and apply the knowledge they have learned.

The progamme is fully immersive and engaging, balancing individual learning with team and wider-group learning experiences. Games and competitions create an element of fun and a sense of community, which powerfully reinforces learning.

It accommodates very large cohorts. This is far more cost effective, as waves of virtual classrooms and one-to-one coaching sessions can be organized at scale. These large cohorts also mean that peer-learning and gamification can be used to greater effect.

The progamme significantly improved worldwide collaboration, problem solving and networking. Following the programme's successful implementation, high participation, positive impact and popular demand, it continues to be delivered and is now being widely rolled out to thousands of associates across the global business. This progamme was awarded first place at the 2016 Learning Technologies Awards for the best blended learning project in the commercial sector and was commended for its impact on the business.

The learner experience

Next generation learning provides users with a single portal from which to conduct all their learning activities. It provides a hub for sharing information and ideas with peers, while cohorts participate in a structured learning journey that blends self-learning with individual challenges and virtual classrooms. This learner-centric approach sees fully flexible custom-built programmes designed not only around the learning and development needs of participants, but also their day-to-day lives. It provides a digital learning spine to permit learners to know exactly where they are on the journey.

Managers are directly involved. They receive nudges to help set learning objectives, provide feedback based on reports throughout the journey and present the learner with their certificate of completion.

100 percent results, zero air miles

It was always predicted that digital would change everything, but until now, as far as learning is concerned, it has been a case of an adolescent masquerading as a grown-up. Now it has come of age. There's been a step change: virtual platforms are more stable, bandwidths wider, software more capable, laptops more powerful, users more accomplished and solutions more evolved. Elearning is actually the old-fashioned sibling to the new power of digital learning, handcuffed by 20th century thinking and, in many ways, masking the true potential of 21st century learning.

In addition to the increased effectiveness of learning that next generation learning programmes provide, the value for organizations is that they can obtain up-to-date reporting from a wealth of data such as real-time participation rates, learning efficacy of specific content and the level of application of learning in the workplace.

Typically, these programmes take a third of the time and half the cost of traditional models of learning, where participants attend a series of face-to-face learning events. Programmes designed this way are more effective. Next generation learning cuts air miles to practically zero. In terms of engagement, we have regularly seen completion and pass rates that are close to 100 percent on even the largest, most ambitious programmes. This is a sea-change for global learning programmes at this scale.

The 12 principles of next generation learning

As a blueprint, we use 12 principles to design next generation learning programmes that deliver tangible strategic outcomes. Each has human and technological implications for transformative learning at scale.

Bespoke learning journeys

Next generation learning programmes enable learners to sequence and structure learning activities to create dynamic learning journeys over time. Participants can access content as and when they want or need it. They can choose their preferred format and depth of learning. Some participants will prefer interactive learning methods, some will prefer one-to-one discussions with a coach or peer, some prefer individual exploration of ideas and examples. The technology recommends learning buddies, further reading and resources, tailored to the needs and requirements of the individual.

Strategic outcomes

Programmes are designed with a clear set of learning outcomes for the individual, closely linked to specific strategic goals of the business. For example, if the strategy requires an improved sales capability, the organization should first define what this specifically means for them; such as having more customers, developing deeper relationships or increasing the speed at which they close deals. They should then translate this into a set of specific competencies, skills and knowledge to be developed through the programme.

Scalable delivery

Next generation learning enables programmatic, transformative learning to be delivered at scale with very large cohorts. A single learning programme could include 5000 people, delivering complex, strategic content in a way that allows individuals to create their own journey to meet their particular learning needs.

The technology platform does all the heavy lifting. It dynamically creates peer communities and learning teams, automates the booking of classrooms and coaching sessions, and keeps participants on track through notifications and reminders. It is also incredibly cost efficient as it applies expert resource as and when needed, using a lean core-delivery team.

Gamified experience

Games and competition are at the heart of next generation learning: from gamifying systems and work to creating simple games that teach complex ideas, business models and insights. Games can be individual or can promote competition between teams. Gamifying the learning experience enables the learner to test ideas in safe scenarios. Next generation learning programmes are designed to reward participation and contribution within an engaging environment.

Connected experts

Huge amounts of expertise already exist in organizations. Often it lies in pockets of excellence, known by some but not easily accessible by many. The challenge is finding and mapping existing expertise so that it can be shared with others as and when needed. As Lew Platt, CEO and chairman of Hewlett-Packard in the 1990s said: 'If only HP knew what HP knows, we would be three times more productive.' Next generation learning programmes create dynamic maps of pre-existing expert knowledge, enabling experts to bubble up in learning communities through their contributions to resource libraries and conversations.

These individuals become mentors and coaches for other participants – and the wider organization.

Personalized learning

Next generation learning programmes are highly personalized, enabling individuals to maximize their available time for training. For example: a personalized learning schedule is created on demand, based on availability; learning teams are formed and personal-development coaches are recommended automatically based on individual's location, role and level of expertise; content is curated based on learning-style preferences and previous knowledge.

Fully flexible

Next generation learning programmes are designed with flexibility in mind, both for the individual learners and the organization. For individuals, the timescale, activities, modes of learning and channels can be tailored to fit around their schedule and their needs. For example, videos or podcasts can be downloaded to a mobile device for access on the commute to work. Virtual classrooms are available almost anytime, as they are arranged to accommodate multiple and global time zones. For organizations, the progamme can be scaled up or down quickly depending on the strategic requirements. This flexibility dramatically increases participation and completion of programmes. The flexibility of these programmes also means that the focus and content can be easily adjusted to stay aligned with any new strategic goals. This level of flexibility would be unthinkable without a digital approach.

Curated content

As with existing expertise, high-quality content is often readily available within organizations. The challenge is to provide curated content for learners together with the resources and conversations most relevant to them. We find that a successful model is to provide just enough useful tools, concepts and examples around a topic, then encourage participants to contribute and share their own best practice and other resources. Participants soon add their own materials, building a dynamic library of curated content for themselves; for example, TED talks, white papers and best-practice cases. Popular resources then bubble up through 'likes', trending features or tags.

Multi-media and multi-channel

In one recent next generation learning program, a participant discussion emerged around 'What was your favourite Sunday evening TV show?' Many responded by saying: 'This learning programme'. Given that participants only have limited time available, content needs to be compelling, entertaining, on demand and relevant. Programmes that provide a full range of media, such as film, games, quizzes and animation, increase engagement and the effectiveness of learning. They need to be available across any device, online and offline, automatically synchronizing across platforms. Participants might book onto a virtual classroom and watch an interactive video tutorial on their journey into work on their mobile device, but then participate in a virtual classroom or learning team at their desktop.

People centred

Digital places learning at the point where learners need it most – in the workplace. It is vital that next generation learning technology platforms facilitate this in an integrated way.

Too often online learning is a technology-led, one-dimensional activity. Research has demonstrated that individuals excel when surrounded by the right support network. Next generation learning programmes put learners at the centre and closely link them with their line manager, a personal coach, peer experts and a learning team. This people ecosystem is motivating, encourages stickiness with the programme and ensures the maximum learning from the experience.

People can achieve remarkable things in a short timeframe when surrounded by relevant expertise. We admire the work in this area of Mihaly Csikszentmihalyi on flow states and learning.

Community based

We are a social species and we learn better when doing so alongside a community of peers. Learning requires experiences that bring people together – learning teams, informal meet-ups, problem solving work groups – to draw people in and engage them with the knowledge around them. An approach like this is key to creating a community of animated learners. Careful design is required to scale this up to engage and animate the learning community over time.

We've highlighted previously a specific role we call the 'community animator.' In a next generation learning programme, the purpose of this role is to build and maintain communities of learners, even long after the formal learning progamme has been completed. Team activities, challenges and games provide opportunities for sharing and collaboration. Community animators actively encourage participation through nudging and connecting the group.

Real-time feedback

Creating effective learning programmes requires rapid and real-time feedback. Dynamic reporting and live feedback provides both the individual and the organization with real-time analysis of the impact of learning. Whilst also demonstrating successes, transparent and consistently available visual feedback enables issues to be identified quickly and trajectories to self-correct.

Conclusion

In rising to the challenge of digital transformation, clearly, organizations cannot expect to replace a traditional, in-depth, face-to-face learning programme by doing nothing more than hosting content in an online library. To achieve results, it has to be about more than just technology. The design, the process, the system and the context of learning all matter: it is about finding a human-centric solution to online learning experiences.

Applying the research of how adults best learn, next generation learning brings together state-of-the-art content, one-to-one coaching and virtual classrooms to create highly personalized learning, for very large cohorts around the world. Everyone can participate and collaborate simultaneously, while at the same time choosing their own preferred path through a programme.

Organizations need to be ready to provide effective learning at a massive scale using digital tools. The culture of the digital organization will be determined by the quality of the learning provided. Providing flexible and highly personalized learning programmes at scale is a strategic imperative for organizations to remain competitive in the rapidly changing business landscape.

The next generation of learning programmes will enable organizations to build the strategic capabilities they require, far faster and more cost effectively than ever before. They will use all the resources of the digital realm to dramatically speed up the cycles of skills building to realize competitive advantage.

We are reaching a point in civilization where every individual on the planet has access to all of the documented knowledge that exists, wherever they may be. The vast knowledge bases of Baghdad and Alexandria are nothing compared to what is now available to every one of us. The skills that enable us to use this information, to make sense of it, and to be able to navigate labyrinths of knowledge with questions and curiosity, will define the behaviours of our next generation.

The way that navigation of the sea was a critical requirement for kingdoms to thrive in the Middle Ages, or agricultural husbandry was critical knowledge for surviving in the pre-industrial age, so too will digital learning skills define success in our age. Everything has changed and nothing has changed.

14.

MEANINGFUL ALTERNATIVES

'Unless someone like you cares a whole awful lot,
Nothing is going to get better. It's not.'

Dr Seuss, *The Lorax*

We explore the ideas and the behaviours that dominate our massively connected global organizations. How to achieve a shift from one state to another – whether it be something more efficient, focused on different outcomes, or operating in new ways. We explore the idea of a dominant mindset of a group and what it takes to transform it when it is a globally connected, amorphous, always changing digital network of different interest groups.

The heretic king

Around 1351 BC, Amenhotep IV ascended the throne of Egypt. Father to Tutankhamun and married to the beautiful Nefertiti, Amenhotep turned out to be a radical pharaoh with radically new ideas. Within a few years of becoming pharaoh, he set about single-handedly changing what he perceived to be Egypt's outdated religious system. Amenhotep decreed that all of Egypt would abandon the millennia old pantheon of gods in favour of a single deity, the sun god Aten. He changed his name to Akhenaten and began systematically removing all signs of the old gods. The pharaoh's new name contained the name of the sun deity and meant 'effective for Aten.'

Akhenaten believed in the power of aligning people around a single, clear and tangible monotheistic doctrine. At the time, more than 1500 old gods were worshipped, each having many representations. Instead of gods such as Nu, the personification of the formless, or Set, Horus, Geb, Mu, Anubis, or Min, who each represented characteristics of the natural and metaphysical worlds. All the personifications of the gods were now attributed to one god, Aten. Aten was the Sun, clearly visible in the sky. The works of Aten could be seen manifest in the daily, monthly and annual cycles in nature. This new religion was defined around the daily cycle of the sun from birth to rebirth, its impact on the fertility of Egypt and its people and the Egyptians' relationship with the waters of the Nile.

Imagine how dramatic a shift this was for the society. Egypt had for thousands of years been pantheistic and animistic. Its economy was hugely tied up with the rituals, festivals and cycles associated with the temples and the gods. The priestly class were the richest and most powerful outside of the royal family. This was a shift in philosophy on every level. Akhenaten decreed that a new form of visual art was required, one that emphasized more natural imagery and informal representations, as distinct from the formal hieroglyphic forms. On his orders, he was himself represented pictorially as a family man with his wife and children, and less as a god. An analogy would be the modern day spiritual leaders of Hinduism decreeing the replacement of the established pantheon of gods by a single god.

Akhenaten also believed that a change in environment would shift mindsets and behaviours. He oversaw the construction of huge new temples and a new divine city named Amarna, a place free of association with the old gods. Despite fierce resistance from the priestly class, most of the elite shifted their allegiance to Akhenaten and tens of thousands of people moved to his new capital. In every respect this was a war on the values, systems, economies, histories and establishment of Egypt. His reforms nearly bankrupted the country and took his attention away from international relations with neighbouring empires. He began losing territory and allegiances. After his sudden death in 1336 BC, his son Tutankhamen declared him a heretic. Tutankhamen re-allied the throne with the old gods and their priests. He restored the old religious customs and had Akhenaten's name chiselled from the walls. Akhenaten's one-man revolution towards a new system was over and its leader was written out of history. The alliance of Tutankhamen with the old order and priestly class may go some way to answering the question of why his tomb was so richly adorned, heaped with gold and brilliantly embellished beyond anything that has ever been unearthed.

For ancient Egyptians, Akhenaten was an idealist and a madman. He set out to make sweeping changes within society and nearly succeeded. He presented a powerful and meaningful alternative, using a combination of policy, environment, doctrine and personal power to shift the mindsets of the people of Egypt. With more time, perhaps his new religion might have caught on and today we would refer to Atenism in the same breath as other monotheistic faiths. However, it was ultimately a failure. His ideas were anathema to the Egyptian establishment. After he had died, the river Nile was redirected away from his city, leaving Amarna to wither and ultimately be forgotten as it was swallowed by the sands of the desert. Leading change is not for the faint hearted.

We can see the impact of digital on everything. It is changing the behaviours of the majority of people on the planet. It is conceivable that every single human, in the not too distant future, will own some kind of smart, connected device. Do we stand at a pivotal point in human history? This is not the first time that new ideas and technologies have had a significant impact on our societies. The impact of the internal combustion engine, urban sanitation, the telephone, television, schooling, universal suffrage, democracy, polio vaccines, are just a few examples of phenomena that have significantly changed the way we live.

However, there is something deeply different about digital. It connects all of us. It is being coded with artificial intelligence. It is becoming clear that there are deep philosophical implications in this shift, most notably the fundamental question about what it means to be human. Society is embracing digital in every way: from the way we spend our time, to the way we work, learn, socialize and play. Will this be our saviour, our downfall or neither?

Digital enables us to do things together on a scale and at a speed that is mind boggling. Decisions are being made collaboratively by millions of autonomous connected individuals. The traditional collective instruments of politics, culture and communication have been radically challenged. Our institutions and parliaments have all been dramatically challenged by this new reality. We are questioning everything while the old guard attempt to cling to power or put the genie back in the bottle. Tim Berners-Lee did warn about this. We need only look at the interest groups who have sought to regulate the Internet and undermine net neutrality in ways that go far beyond the protection of vulnerable individuals. The Internet cannot be switched off as some would like. Its mechanisms, impact and benefits have been hard wired into the fabric of our societies and organizations. It has become the principal way that business is done and accounted for. There is no going back.

With this in mind, we have to ask: What are we looking to achieve? What are the meaningful alternatives we are creating and how should we step into this future with intention? As leaders, how do we influence these new digital global organizations? How do we ensure we create a future that everyone wants – a meaningful alternative – so as not to become the architects of our own destruction and avoid a similar fate to Akhenaten?

The golden age of Athens

Winding the clock forward about 1000 years, the golden age of Athens in the 5th century BC was inspired by a revolutionary shift in mindset towards democracy and towards the greater involvement of citizens within the state. We still see lasting influences of that vision around the world today and physically in the Acropolis that dominates the Athenian skyline.

These ideas were inspired by Pericles, a brilliant orator and general who dominated public life as 'the first citizen of Athens' for 40 years.

A populist and a patron of the arts and literature, Pericles had a vision for a fully democratic and magnificent Athens.

His was an inspiring vision that allowed him to unite much of Greece under the influence of Athens. 'Demos' in 'democratic' means 'common people' and Pericles led social innovations that opened up Athens to all of its people. He subsidized theatre admission and paid for a civil service. He is also famed for the series of buildings that sit atop the Acropolis, most notably the Parthenon. When it was constructed, its scale, magnificence and cost scandalized the world at the time. The genius of Pericles was to create a monument to democracy that had at its heart the god whom the Athenians revered above all. It was proclaimed as a lasting monument to the greatness of Athena, the goddess of Athens. He linked these two ideas in a way that ensured the Athenians (and the Athenian league) were on board, were inspired by it and agreed to pay for it.

In his famous funeral oration for Pericles, Thucydides reports him as having said: 'Our polity does not copy the law of neighbouring states; we are rather a pattern to others than imitators ourselves. It is called a democracy because it is governed not by the few but by the many.'

The results of this democratic shift in mindset still influence us today. Unlike Akhenaten, Pericles found a way to not only describe a compelling vision for the future but also to take the people along with him. Through the power of his storytelling he transformed the city of Athens and did so by involving the people in its realization. The golden age of Athens inspired a way of life that has lasted for thousands of years.

To transform our societies, cultures and organizations, we need to create meaningful alternatives for ourselves as digital humans. This will require a vision inspiring enough to make individuals truly want to see it realized and motivating enough for them to want to be part of building it. In such a time of uncertainty and change in our society, what can we learn from the failures and the successes of visionaries such as Akhenaten and Pericles to ensure meaningful and lasting change?

A meaningful alternative

'I think it would be great to be born on Earth and die on Mars. Just hopefully not at the point of impact.'

Elon Musk

Elon Musk is perhaps a modern-day Pericles. A self-made billionaire, an orator in our digital age and currently one of the world's most influential people. Musk fires our imagination with his ideas for the future. He creates visual events — such as placing a Tesla car in the nose cone of a test rocket launched into space — that portray his vision for our future society. From electric cars to hyperloops, high-speed transportation and fully battery powered energy plants, Musk's businesses address challenges that he believes will most affect the future of humanity. His work focuses on sustainable energy, transportation, the Internet and space exploration. An expert promoter, he knows the power of digital to engage the imagination of every human on the planet. Like Pericles' Acropolis, he stages grand events to inspire and focus the attention and knows how to bring the people along with him.

In March 2016, Musk announced publicly that Tesla's batteries could solve South Australia's chronic summer power-outage problems. He made a bet on Twitter that his company could, in just 100 days, build a 129 MWh lithium ion battery system in South Australia. This would be the biggest anywhere in the world. If Tesla failed to meet the deadline, Australia would get its money back, no questions asked. Tesla succeeded and Musk won the bet.

Perhaps the most impressive of Musk's ventures is SpaceX. Founded in 2002, SpaceX has the 'ultimate goal of enabling people to live on other planets'. Whilst not a new idea, Musk's company is actively building it and has the capital backing to do so. Launching rockets in space is a famously difficult and dangerous business and SpaceX has had many challenges and setbacks, but as Musk says: 'You should take the approach that you're wrong. Your goal is to be less wrong.'

Elon Musk and his ventures are bringing into reality things we thought were impossible or decades away. The digital transformation that is currently taking place offers the same unthought of possibilities. With digital, we no longer have to build new cities or physical monuments, to fire the imagination and bring to life a new alternative reality. We can create powerful and immersive stories that extend their reach into every part of the organization in a deeply personal way. As we have described throughout this book, digital means we can engage every individual in being part of building that future together.

Motivating digital humans

Every community, tribe or organization has a dominant mindset, a mental attitude that impacts every aspect of it. That mindset determines how an organization and its people interpret and respond to different situations. At times of change, its significance should not be underestimated.

If the dominant mindset has been forged during difficult or uncertain times, when people feel apathy, negativity or trepidation, it can derail even the most sophisticated and meticulously planned of transformation projects. Identifying the mindset of your organization and making efforts to shift it is, then, critical to the success or failure of any change.

The scientist and systems analyst Donella Meadows observed that there are places within every complex system (be it a business, a city or an economy) where 'a small shift in one thing can produce big changes in everything.' As we described earlier, we can see the power of these small things in everything from the game of Go to the introduction of lavender and roses in vineyards to reduce the need for pesticides.

Meadows, whose own research focused on the environmental limits to economic growth, proposed a sliding scale of points at which to intervene in a system, ranked from least to most effective. At the top, the point where a small shift can make the greatest change, Meadows put 'the mindset or paradigm out of which the system arises.'

Take, for a recent example, the attractions of a healthy lifestyle, which has now taken hold of the public's imagination. In the 1960s and 1970s, the standard might have been set by professional footballers who were happy to have a smoke and a lager at half time. Today's top sportsmen and women are now uncompromising elite athletes, continually in pursuit of peak fitness and performance.

The compelling future that surrounds us, echoed in media and advertising, is not just a healthy old age, but of health and fitness throughout our lives. We can see the promise all around us. When people have access to the latest information, support and role models, with their behaviours reinforced by digital tools, they are living longer, healthier lives.

Meaning motivates us as humans. We need to feel we are invested in a future narrative that offers more than where we are now. Throughout history we have inspired ourselves by creating narratives, myths and stories that take us forward across the abyss of the unknown.

The narrative and stories that are told within an organization's culture can be the difference between those that are highly motivated and agile, and those that are not. Organizations that have been through tough times need to work harder to shift the dominant mindset and create new stories, establishing a reinvigorated set of narratives that are compelling and motivating. In our work, we have found that there are three particularly effective methods that can be applied to develop a meaningful alternative and engage the digital organizational system in doing so.

Co-create the alternative

A new vision for the future can come from one individual, but more successfully and more powerfully from many. To create this shared vision we recommend engaging with teams from different areas, innovative thinkers and also the wider ecosystem. It's important to do this early in the process. By first understanding the context, then learning and working together, more sophisticated thinking emerges. This improves the quality of the ideas and begins the process of engaging people in the change from the start. As we have described, digital tools make it far easier to engage people to contribute ideas from right across the organization: With the right tools and processes, highly creative, facilitated visioning events can be run entirely online without the need for costly facilities and travel time. The alternative needs to be inspiring, on a massive scale, challenging and something we all want to be a part of.

Create memorable experiences

Touch the hearts and minds of people with memorable experiences that bring the vision to life. What is the new future you have designed and what will it do for people? How can it be made tangible in such a way they people believe it is possible to achieve? What are the grand monuments and projects that can be created, and how can they involve as many people as possible in their construction? One example could be to make a documentary movie. Working with film experts and people from all parts of the organization, describe the future through scenarios and practical examples – with the stars of the show being the people who will be part of making it happen. The tools available to us today mean that films with very high production standards can be made far faster and cheaper than before.

Recognize and reinforce the new world

Every cause needs its disciples: those people who are passionate about the future vision and willing to share their passion with others. Role models are required who already exhibit the qualities, ways of working and mindset that we want to make manifest in the future. The way that we choose to inject the new skills and abilities required by the future organization is of paramount importance. If we make the new ways of working easier, better or more enjoyable than the old, the likelihood of defaulting back to old ways is much less. Take particular care and effort to clarify how individual's work contributes to organizational goals and be quick to reward desired behaviours. As the journey moves forward, continually reinforce that we are on the right track by sharing success and celebrating victories, large and small.

Putting it into practice: the future of finance

A global company was looking to shift from a regional to a global finance function. It was a bold and ambitious vision, one that would require complete shifts in culture, ways of working, skills, behaviours and technology.

Initially we worked with the global finance leadership team, taking them through an intensive facilitated week-long experience. It brought together their ideas and experiences from right across the globe. A blueprint for the future was created together. Nobody wanted to destabilize the existing organization but everybody wanted to design a future that accelerated growth. The leaders wanted to ensure that the future financial organization supported the global strategic vision and maximized value across the entire ecosystem. They needed to create a collaborative vision that they could all sign up to. This meant working through all the obstacles that they could perceive and being inspired by what they could achieve together for the good of all.

The next step was to engage the finance community of 3000 finance professionals from across more than 50 countries of operation in the vision. The intention was to enable everyone in the organization to have a voice in developing the strategy and the desired culture. It was important to provide the opportunity for conversation and constructive engagement for everyone to understand for themselves what was required to think, work and act differently. Candid feedback was encouraged and shared across all areas of the business.

A collaboration portal was set up through which participants could set their own preferences for how they wanted to engage. A series of more than 50 virtual workshops were held, facilitated by peers from within the business. Conversations and ideas were shared to allow for as many parallel conversations as possible.

In less than six weeks, thousands of people from around the world had provided feedback on the proposed vision and the challenges of realizing it. All associates made personal commitments to own or support a project that would help to deliver the strategy. Everybody was asked to identify and make a conscious change to just one of their own behaviours (such as to connect more regularly with colleagues around the world). People were engaged in teams to work through scenarios and problem-solve challenges relating to the vision.

At each stage, associates could contribute, comment, vote and receive real-time feedback through the tool. Throughout the process, everyone could see the aggregated results of all the challenges, solutions and commitments. These were then brought together into a final set of insights for analysis, synthesis and visualization. Now the business had a roadmap, based on every associate's input. This allowed the global leadership to understand which initiatives to prioritize to maximize the development of the new culture, as well as how to determine which new processes and technology to implement. This process and its outputs became the clear means for delivering the vision.

As a result, the global finance function now has an influential 'seat at the table' in the wider organization. Seen as real partners in negotiations with suppliers and advisors in strategic decision-making, the programme shifted the mindsets of associates and with that the perceptions of the wider business. The function has also forged far stronger links between different geographies, shortcutting much of the past bureaucracy.

Conclusion

As humans, many possible futures are open to us. They can inspire us or they can alarm us. We don't have to leap into the future all at once. We can iterate towards it by creating a vision and a narrative, then starting small, building on the positives and learning to make demands on the system as it emerges to do things in a new way.

Our digital world enables us to explore a new state before actually requiring the system to make the shift. Through a continuous exploration and testing of reality, change becomes meaningful and desired without becoming stressful. The use of methods such as prototypes, design thinking, collaborative testing and digital scenario-building enables massive global groups to create compelling future states that they everyone wants to be connected with.

15.

TURN IT ON

'From a little spark may burst a flame.'

Dante Alighieri

This chapter is about the power of stories to build movements. Stories sit at the heart of the history of our species in the way we make decisions and how we engage our tribes in the digital realm. We also recommend options for communication and engagement with virtual communities.

The gates of paradise

In 1401 in Florence, a competition was announced. The Arte di Calimala (the wool merchants' guild), one of the wealthiest in the city, invited local artists to compete for the commission of the Florence Baptistery's eastern doors. Having been ravaged by the plague, like most of Europe, the city was finally ready for a new beginning.

Seven artists participated in the competition. Every artist had to design and submit a trial piece, a quatrefoil panel depicting the binding of Isaac using a small amount of bronze. The competition was narrowed down to Lorenzo Ghiberti and Filippo Brunelleschi, their work being adjudged the most impressive by far. The committee suggested that they work together on the doors. Brunelleschi refused, leaving Ghiberti as the outright winner.

Ghiberti's bronze doors comprise 28 panels, with 20 panels depicting the story of the life of Christ as described in the New Testament. It took 21 years to complete. In 1425 Ghiberti was subsequently commissioned to design a second pair of bronze doors for the Baptistery containing 10 stories, this time from the Old Testament. He worked on these doors for 27 years, creating a masterpiece even more beautiful than the first. His original doors were moved from the east to the north entrance to make way for his new works to take prominence at the eastern side of the Baptistery. They were a masterpiece. Michelangelo himself considered these doors to be 'truly worthy to be the gates of paradise' for their remarkable beauty and grandeur. Ghiberti's ideas were radical. He led the way for the artist to be seen as an important figure in society and the role of art in defining culture and cultural change.

Many historians point to this competition and Ghiberti's doors as the dawn of the Renaissance. A pivotal moment between the old and the new that led to a period of remarkable creativity and cultural change. The Renaissance was one of the most profound movements of aesthetics, culture and learning in the history of Europe.

Create a movement

Today, anyone of the billions of people on the planet can start a movement that spreads like wildfire. We see it every day, from protests and uprisings to social media frenzies. Sometimes these are deliberate; often these are simply ideas that capture the popular imagination and go viral. Think of the #timesup movement that is defining our current moment.

Digital organizations can accelerate change within themselves by creating movements that grow organically. The question is how do organizations create the spark for sustainable change in the longer term? How can they use the power of their tribes to shift the organization from the inside? Perhaps Elon Musk's public bet that his firm could create a battery to solve South Australia's power outage problem (see the previous chapter) will be seen in time as a doing for the age of renewables what the Florentine competition of 1401 did for the Renaissance?

In our experience, there are three main ingredients to turning an organization on to change. These are:

- A compelling story

- An activated community

- A multi-layered campaign

We look at how organizations can use each to turn their change programmes into movements.

A compelling story

'Life changes in the instant. The ordinary instant.
We tell ourselves stories in order to live.'

Joan Didion

Every individual on the planet is a natural born storyteller. It's ingrained in our psyche. As digital humans, we are sharing stories with more people and more frequently than ever before in history. Every role in every community shares stories as part of living and transforming - the shaman, the medic, the chief, the warrior, the mother. These storytelling roles continue to exist today, but in the digital world, the storytelling reaches far greater audiences.

A compelling narrative can transcend a product, propel a brand into consumers' lives and forge deep emotional connections. One of the reasons that Ghiberti's *Gates of Paradise* are forever popular, over and above their exquisite beauty and craftsmanship, is the story told within each panel of the doors.

From our earliest origins, it is our stories that have bound us together as communities. Nothing reinforces changing patterns of behaviour and languages as powerfully as stories. Stories reach the parts that logic cannot reach, and no great leader has ever been blind to the power of a story to create trust, value and purpose. Their appeal lies deep within us.

Storytelling appeals to the limbic part of our brains, where hearts are won and where, often unconsciously, value judgements are made that exert a strong influence on our behaviour and mindset. If we are told a story, we are more likely to relate to it, bringing to bear our own experiences, memories, emotions and imaginations. Information in the abstract is much harder to absorb. Humans are literally transformed by stories.

Massive change is upon us. And there's nothing quite like the threat of change to test the courage, confidence and competence of leaders. If leadership is partly about inspiring a community of individuals to undertake a collective endeavour, then stories are essential to articulate that vision. Noel Tichy in his book *The Leadership Engine* remarks that: 'The best way to get humans to venture into unknown terrain is to make that terrain familiar and desirable by taking them there first in their imagination'.

When a leader inspires, he or she breathes life and energy into their followers. As Antoine de Saint-Exupéry remarked: 'If you want to build a ship, don't drum up the men to gather wood, divide the work and give orders. Instead teach them to yearn for the vast and endless sea.' When we reflect on the extraordinarily motivating speeches Churchill made, it's clear that no amount of slideware (had it existed) and no amount of consultancy or accountancy modelling would ever have had the power of his well-chosen words. Martin Luther King had a dream, he didn't have a change goal and wasn't at a critical point of inflection.

Powerful stories begin with a powerful idea. In the world of story, writers refer to the 'controlling idea' of the narrative. What is the intention or reason for telling a story? What is it about?

We can find the intention behind our story by being clear about why we are telling it. Stories can be used to inspire, motivate, develop, influence, engage, bring insights, gain commitment or connect to others. They can be used in the context of leading, learning, selling or sharing. To tell a powerful story means first getting the intention right and then getting the audience to listen. Nothing hooks an audience like telling a story that comes from a place of truth.

Bringing stories to life requires art. All art requires us to expose ourselves, whether we are using words, visual media, sculpture, drama, music or even dance. Skillful storytellers don't shy away from combining the right blend of these in service of their message. There will be a sense of presence and performance to their story so that it comes alive, becomes something the audience wants to hear again and is memorable enough to retell to others.

One of the most successful channels on YouTube has been the TED talks. A powerful source of new ideas told by inspirational people. These individuals are asked to tell 'the story of their lives' and in so doing connect their passion with the emotions of the audience. The channel is compelling and informative.

Stories transform organizations. Storytelling gives organizations the power to build momentum from the bottom up as well as from the top down. Stories can be used to describe a future state, reinforce results or share knowledge. Here are five ways we use stories to enable organizations to transform.

Bring the vision to life

Stories help people make sense of change, revealing the reasons behind it and highlighting the need for a new organizational vision. In the abstract, strategy can seem far removed from the day to day. Through stories, it can be brought to life, framing change in ways that enhances its credibility and instilling confidence that it can be achieved.

Build emotional connections

Storytelling creates strong emotional connections between a tribe. A tribe is defined by the stories it tells. At a time of change, when many are feeling apprehensive, such positive personal connections can make a significant difference, particularly when they are being asked to adopt new values, attitudes or behaviours.

Amplify excellence

Change will inevitably generate feelings of discontent or concerns about underperformance. These can hold back transformation as people naturally resist what is uncomfortable or difficult. Rather than allow negative rumours to take hold, it pays to actively encourage the spread of stories of excellence and success that are already happening. Sharing success stories mean these ideas are transmitted in a way that encourages energy and engagement. People typically like to share good news. They unleash best practices that already exist and reinforce conversations about new behaviours, perspectives and ideas.

Increase participation

Transformations often stall, not through a lack of willingness, but because of an uncertainty about how to engage. By putting in place simple mechanisms, such as an online forum, everyone is given the chance to contribute. It enables individuals to focus their energy and contribute in a meaningful and productive way.

Improve internal communication

People respond well when the stories they have shared are seen to be followed up on by leaders and influencers. People want to be heard and valued. Structured storytelling, whether through digital 'fireside chats', face-to-face meetings, online discussion forums or traditional broadcast events, co-creates the changes required. We engage with the new narratives and apply our own experience to the message.

In the digital age, those who can tell the best stories will win. From start-ups to insurgents everywhere new stories are the high ground from which to shake assumptions and overthrow the established order. Their power lies less in their command of assets and resources but in their ability to capture the popular imagination. They are using the digital platforms to create movements, campaigns and insurrections that upend the establishment.

An activated community

'Whatever you do will be insignificant, but it is very important that you do it.'

Mahatma Gandhi

Lysistrata was an amazing woman and the main protagonist of Aristophane's best loved comedy. It is the story of one woman's incredible mission to end the Peloponnesian War. In the 5th century BC play, she organized the Athenian women to agree not to have sex with their husbands and lovers until they sued for peace and ended the interminable war. The women are dubious and reluctant at first, but the deal is sealed with a long and solemn oath around a wine bowl: 'I shall stay in my home, untouchable, in my finest Amorgan silk and make him long for me.' Through her own sense of individual responsibility and determination, Lysistrata creates a powerful movement and through the community of women of Athens, succeeds in stopping the war.

In his 1971 manifesto *Rules for Radicals*, Saul Alinsky described 13 rules for changing an organization from within. These included 'never going outside the expertise of your people', 'a good tactic is one your people enjoy' and 'keep the pressure on'. For us, however, his most important principle, as Lysistrata used to such great effect, was to start from where people are currently, with what is most important to them, not from where you want them to be.

Currently of course social media is being used (and abused) to build communities that create a tidal wave of change. The revolutions in Tunisia and Egypt that led to the Arab Spring and the riots in England in 2011 were sparked by social media. #BlackLivesMatter is a campaign against violence and racism. The #MeToo campaign is directed against sexual assault and harassment, especially in the workplace.

As we have described previously, humans have evolved as social animals motivated by being part of a community or tribe. We are instinctively bound by the values, identities and stories that we share. Our communities, even in our highly-evolved state, still work best on an almost tribal basis of reciprocal trust.

213

For anyone now seeking to right a wrong, launching a business or transforming an organization, the same principles apply. In evolutionary terms, we put ourselves at a significant advantage by building a movement and activating trust in communities. As was said by Stephen M.R. Covey: business moves at the speed of trust. Think how easily and swiftly things can get done with trust. He calls it 'the key leadership competency of the new global economy'.

Building trust within and among different tribes is vital to successfully maintain the integrity of global organizations. Trust keeps us together, keeps us focused and enables us to be successful together, no matter how far apart we may live around the world.

Building communities of trust

In economics, it is usually assumed that we act as egotists in our rational self-interest. So why, then, are so many of us inclined towards co-operating in communities of trust? It is a question that took Elinor Ostrom to the Nobel Prize - the first and, so far, only female economist to have won.

She was a pioneer in developing a theory around the everyday reality that co-operation among individuals is widespread, if not inevitable. As she presented in *Governing the Commons: The Evolution of Institutions for Collective Action*, steps have to be taken against the temptation to free ride on the provision of collective benefits.

She observed that some individuals were more likely than others to take part in collective action. So how could they identify one another and build communities of trust? Why are variations so great in the level of co-operation in different social settings?

The challenge within a common pool of resources, she found, was that individuals must balance an instinct for their own free use of resources against controls that keep it fair. In Garrett Hardin's 1968 essay *The Tragedy of the Commons*, he describes this challenge perfectly. Hardin tells a parable of villagers adding too many cows to their common pasture. The farmer who added an extra cow gained an advantage over other farmers in his village, but his action also led to an overgrazed pasture. If we draw on our understanding of evolution and recognize the principle of reciprocity that was an integral part of our early social development, we can create a system based on rules that lead to greater trust.

Ostrom advises that everyone gets a say in setting the rules and selecting their own supervisors who can apply a graduated set of sanctions for non-cooperation. As the scale of co-operation intensifies, more formal methods for resolving disputes are introduced. Eventually, a series of small nested organizations will emerge within an overarching structure. The Venetian Guilds emerged to govern the various crafts in a similar way.

Collective action within trusted communities can lead to a series of social benefits. However, attempts to encourage them by policy-makers are often misdirected. They struggle to break free from our economic norms, relying on 'pay-off structures for rational egotists'. Instead Ostrom recommends 'increasing the authority of individuals to devise their own rules'. It is the activating of these communities of trust to implement new ideas and to share stories that is of vital importance for leaders of change.

Creating activists

If we live in a world in which digital disruptors and social activists can easily seize power, what can we learn from how these activists succeed? How can we harness the passion and enthusiasm of tribes? How can we build movements within our organizations to capture the imagination of a workforce whose attention is under siege from everything?

As we learn from Gandhi, the first rule for any movement is to be clear about the objective. His coalition harboured many and various grievances against the Raj. He narrowed the disgruntlement to a single grievance and campaign: a peaceful protest against the salt tax. From there, he had the British Empire on the wrong foot, until it eventually accepted the case for independence.

In winning over potential supporters, allies and customers, it helps to identify a common cause. Against whom or for what are we uniting?

How can we identify our campaign or tribe in opposition?

As we start to push out the message, we must expect our opponents to push back and to present rising levels of resistance. However, in organizational change, we are trying to win arguments, not start a war. So how can we co-opt our adversaries? They are the ones with the power to make change happen.

So, pay attention to choosing the cause well. Start-ups ignite interest around a problem they are solving as crowdfunding companies such as Kickstarter demonstrate. Breathing life into projects such as the Pebble Time and the card game Exploding Kittens, they create an idea with which people can emotionally connect and communicate with passion. The features of the product still matter, of course, but what really counts is the level of engagement and emotional excitement around the experience they offer.

To build a common purpose, we bring together people who share the same passion as us. The importance of being a leader of a movement is over-glorified. Fame is irrelevant here. The most important people are those first followers who then activate their networks. They have the power to transform the lone voice into a leader of tribes. Change will start when those first followers and activists try and do something new and then talk to their friends about it. From there, those first followers entrain other people to do the same thing. So it goes viral.

To create followers, leaders need to create a sense of shared purpose in their teams, their network and their organization. Despite popular myth, a ragtag of revolutionaries rarely achieves anything on a large scale. Social activists need to know how to behave on the frontline or at a demo. Otherwise they will soon be rounded up.

In the digital age, movements are built through a connected series of small groups. The moment will come for the movement to march en masse. But the network needs to be put in place first. For start-ups, it can take time to identify the characteristics of those who can spread out and tell the story. For leaders, the work is to go out and speak to people in real life, find the people who can activate the organization and give them the digital tools to do so.

A multi-layered campaign

'You say you want a revolution
Well, you know
We all want to change the world'

Revolution, The Beatles

Transformation often loses momentum as it begins to scale. It is important to create specific opportunities for individuals to stay engaged in the change to maintain momentum and harness the best thinking across the organization in a structured way.

To capture the hearts and minds of time-pressed, media-savvy digital humans, state-of-the-art engagement needs to be multi-channel and multi-media. When done well, a campaign is packed full of memorable experiences and narratives. These campaigns enable new models and new language that describe the future state to be amplified. Think of some of the most impactful advertising campaigns of recent years. The sportswear company Under Armour, for example, has become almost ubiquitous. They equip elite sports people from every discipline, are embedded in many fitness and nutrition apps and even deliver a personalized experience for their customers through their own shopping app. They create a complete multi-channel experience. A similar approach is relevant for organizations looking to harness the power of their tribes.

We define four methods to organize and deliver content with a multi-layered campaign. These methods are: broadcast, cascade, emergent and generative. The best campaigns will have elements of each, to transmit to the broadest possible audience in a meaningful way.

Broadcast

Broadcast can be thought of as a top-down approach. When the priority is to be 100 percent consistent with messaging and content, a broadcast is the best option. Communications at scale across the organization can bring new goals into focus, establish a new visual

217

identity or improve understanding of where the business is going. Typically, we recommend using pre-designed media such as websites, documentaries, presentations, films and old-fashioned print media. Augmented reality and interactive signage are now adding to the impact that these messages have.

Cascade

A cascade is an efficient method for moving and processing information throughout an organization in a systematic way. For a cascade, role models or ambassadors take a lead in giving a visible demonstration of the new requirements and entraining how the organization will change. Entrainment is about promoting synchronous harmonization between people. For example, when someone starts to tap their foot to a musical beat, others will follow. Empathy between people is obvious when we start to copy each other's body language. These role models have to be consistent, personal and passionate in what they do. They bring change to life for large audiences, perhaps through roadshows, online events, workshops or online forums.

Emergent

An emergent approach is one that focuses on synthesis and sharing. A good example would be using best practices already established within the organization to find and amplify pockets of excellence and success stories. Create stories that energize and motivate the target audience. Use design events, whether physical or online, for groups to share and refine the best ideas. These can be encoded into next generation learning programmes to build capability and reinforce new ways of working in the organization. Toolkits for promoting new practices throughout a tribe are a good example of this.

Generative

A generative approach gives people the chance to build the narrative themselves. Starting from the smallest seeds, individuals are encouraged to grow new ideas and solutions. This technique is particularly useful when the goal is to shift the culture and the mindset. This can be done through constructive events, decision apps, online platforms, competitions and collaborative film-making. Instead of just playing a game, people are encouraged to design a game, build it and have others play it. Ideas are allowed to spontaneously develop and scale, often working alongside emergent techniques that allow for editing and synthesis. Design thinking is a very good example of a generative way of working.

Designing a multi-layered campaign

In designing a campaign, we recommend making it highly visual and interactive, blending a number of collaborative technologies and interactive designs to win over and inspire the audience. Use digital tools to develop and track each person's participation to understand the impact. This can be done gathering a rich blend of data about progress, priorities and perceptions. We include elements such as:

- Rich pictures and infographics: visual storytelling devices that translate complex systems, ideas and challenges into clear, powerful images that are easy to understand. These are highly visible, online or wherever people may be working.

- Digital and visual scribing: capture ideas, insights and decisions as they happen live at events or at meetings, online or face-to-face.

- Films and animations: these can immerse, engage and connect the audience, as well as allow people to become active participants in the story.

- Mixed reality tools, such as virtual and augmented reality: these provide a completely immersive experience of the ideas and solutions.

- Collaborative design events: these can be delivered in person or online to accelerate alignment and decision-making or to co-design new solutions.

- Data analytics: insights and feedback that can be captured in real time and displayed visually and on dashboards.

- Games and simulations: these engage an audience in a way that transforms content into play, reinforcing their experience.

- Companion tools: these contain all the knowledge required for specific roles in an accessible, media rich toolkit.

- ebooks, emagazines and microsites: these create interactive, immersive and engaging information experiences for audiences.

In practice: turning around employee engagement

A major supplier of IT services was experiencing a dip in performance. At such moments, negative voices are often those that are heard loudest and most persistently. A sense of apathy was starting to infect its workforce of 11,000 to the point that as many employees felt disengaged as engaged. There was enormous scope to improve.

In response, a campaign was launched to turn up the volume on what was going well. It first sought examples of best practice and other pockets of excellence, then amplified them across the business through multi-channel communications.

Pride was restored by sharing success stories and training was given in the art of telling them. A competition was included to encourage employees to write in a creative and interesting way.

The campaign first focused on defining the business in the way that people wanted. Then to transform it, make it a great place to work and hit financial targets.

These programmes around storytelling and motivational narratives were instrumental in shifting the organization's culture and dominant mindset. With an overall 12 percent increase in employee engagement (and up to 22 percent increase in some business areas), the company started seeing year-on-year growth of 25 percent, with 10 percent growth in orders placed and an increase in return on sales from 4.3 percent to 5.8 percent.

In the next wave, leaders within the business were trained in how to become the authors of their own scripts and to include storytelling in all their forms of communication. This 2½ day course is now in its sixth year.

Conclusion

In the digital age, everyone has the power to share their own stories and create their own movements. Organizations that seek to transform themselves digitally, come up against two primitive threats: disruptors from outside the tribe offering a more compelling narrative; and distractions for their people who have multiple stories from which to choose.

Conventionally, organizations invest heavily in working with outsiders to re-write their strategy or re-position their brand. We suggest that with the right tools and approach, it is now possible for these organizations to call on the power that lies within them. Organizations can build their own camp fires, open up their own flow of stories, create their own movements, enthuse their own workforces and win the trust of their people to activate and transform their organizations from the inside.

Small nudges, and programmes that capture people's attention, like Lysistrata's own #justsayno movement, will scale and define the identity of the change. We're all in it together.

AFTERWORD

'It had long since come to my attention that people of accomplishment rarely sat back and let things happen to them. They went out and happened to things.'

Leonardo da Vinci

The future for digital humans is both exciting and concerning. It offers freedoms we have not had before. We can do less tedious work and be more creative. We can connect with each other and travel more. On the other hand, jobs are at threat from digital automation and our role as humans in this new digital society is unclear. Will we have friendly AI or robots that threaten our existence?

Digital transformation represents a profound shift in how organizations operate and how we lead our lives. It is both extraordinarily exciting in its implications and unnerving for anyone in the middle of it, whose job and whose future are in danger of being superseded.

Against this backdrop, the extent to which those working in organizations will invest themselves and their identities will depend on how compelling they find the stories and futures with which they are presented. If we are to manage the transfer to becoming digital humans with positive outcomes, then a meaningful alternative to the existing system has to be created.

For all the dystopian fears and predictions, we (the writers) continue to be excited and fascinated by the revolution we are privileged enough to be living through. We have referenced historical moments of enormous impact throughout this book, grand and profound change in days long gone. We realize that the passage of time may have focused the significance of those events in a way the people who lived through them may not have fully appreciated. The question that remains foremost in our minds is: are we digital humans today like those people who experienced the industrial revolution without realizing how consequential it would be?

When we say we are excited about future possibilities, it is because we are at a point in human history more extraordinary and remarkable than anything that has gone before. Why should the dystopian theorists be right? As we are still masters of our own destiny, why not roll up our collective sleeves and proactively build the future we all desire?

This book has been our way of sharing with you some of the insight and tools we have encountered thus far on our journey into the digital future. More than anything else it is an attempt to share some of the ways that we believe we can harness digital for the wider good.

There is no doubt that the future of humanity is inextricably bound up with our technology — and as much as we are alive, so it is alive. We evolve together. Like the discovery of all new worlds, let's explore together. Safe in the understanding that through our collective organizations we are responsible for crafting the future we desire for each and every one of us. This way we will create lives that are richer in experience, more fun, connected and ... Alive!

TERMS OF ART

'The difference that makes the difference.'

Gregory Bateson

These terms of art are the definitions of the main terms that we have used writing this book. They are presented in the order we thought of them. The definitions may not be the same as the ones you might provide, however this is the point. As anthropologist Gregory Bateson pointed out in 1972, it is the difference that makes the difference. We welcome your additions and your constructive points of view.

Digital
This is the new technological frontier where value, exchange and relationships are to be found. It changes the boundaries of traditional organizations and creates an entirely new field on which to operate.

Technology
The application of scientific knowledge and engineering for practical purposes. In our use of the term, technology can range from computers and software algorithms to process knowledge. A stirrup on a horse is technology that gave the Mongols a strategic advantage.

Mass media
Multiple technologies that reach a very large population. It includes television, newspapers, magazines, social media and the Internet. Bigger than The Beatles.

Work
The amount of energy required to move something. Something humans either need to do and have to do. Something we hope robots will do for us in the future whilst we humans get to have fun, make love, write poetry and play Go.

Human
Modern humans are members of the sub-tribe Hominina, a branch of the tribe Hominid in the family of great apes.

Digital Human
Any online human. A human being that sees digital as an extension of their everyday life.

Society
A group of humans in constant communication to create an identity and culture, or sharing the same geography, or online territory, subject to similar laws and with similar cultural expectations.

Automation
The use of technology and control systems to replace work that was historically done by humans.

Virtual
Something that doesn't physically exist. This may explain the lack of effectiveness of some virtual teams.

Virtual reality
A simulated reality created by computers, software and apps. Possibly where many of us will start spending a lot of time once robots take over our jobs.

Swarming
The collective behaviour and intelligence of artificial, self-organizing, decentralized simple agents – that operate according to simple rules of interaction.

Synthesize
To create something new by combining different elements, objects or ideas.

Organization
A group of people who gather together with a common purpose or function.

Ecosystem
A complex network of information, people, customers, suppliers and technology. A community made up of living organisms.

Ludic (pron. /ˈluːdɪk/)
Spontaneous or undirected playfulness.

Scale
The capacity of a system to grow rapidly and take on increasing amounts of work.

Transformation
Radical change in order to increase capability or achieve new outcomes.

Decision-making
The activity of resolving a question. Sometimes the experience of going around and around in circles until the most senior person makes their mind up and tells everyone what the answer is.

Collaboration
Working together to achieve more than can be achieved on one's own.

Meeting
Typically a soul-crushing experience popular in the 1990s. Now usually joined via conference call whilst doing something else.

Principle
A proposition that serves to inform beliefs or behaviours. For example, peak-learning principles are a set of beliefs for how to accelerate learning.

Activate
To make something active. To stimulate something new.

Internet
The global system of interconnected computers and networks. Now replaced by 'online' (see below).

Online
Being connected to or controlled by a computer. Digital humans are typically online more often than they are not.

Utopia
An imaginary society that possesses desirable and idealistic characteristics – a perfect society.

Identity
How a person or group defines themselves.

Security
Free from danger or threat.

Tribe
Communities or families that are linked by economics, beliefs, relationships, dialectics, history or culture.

System
A set of things working together, whether people, technology or objects.

Living system
Open self-organizing life forms that interact with their environment. These systems are maintained by flows of information, energy and matter.

Complex systems
Any system with a very large set of intersecting components whose outcomes are achieved non-linearly.

Methodology
A body of rules, practices and methods that define a type of work.

Model
A representation of a set of ideas created in visual format for aiding memory.

Platform
A raised level surface on which people can stand. A piece of software upon which other pieces of software can run.

Simple rules
A short set of instructions that should be easy to follow and lead to complex behaviour. Similar to flat packed furniture manuals.

Jazz
A form of music that emerged at the beginning of the 20th century, known for its use of improvisation around a main beat. Typically, something that humans either love or hate.

Labyrinth
A connected set of pathways that are deliberately designed to be difficult to traverse. A maze.

Consultant
A person who gives professional advice.

Iteration
The process of improving something by testing and re-making it.

Design
A plan or drawing of something to be created. A matter of personal taste.

Design thinking
The method by which designers solve problems.

Culture
The ideas, customs and behaviours of a particular group.

Leadership
Motivating others to achieve a common goal.

Innovation
Bringing a new idea into reality.

Brainstorming
A series of exercises for generating ideas in which intuitive tools are often used.

Framework
The supporting structure of a building or object. A set of concepts that inform how to act.

Network
We very much like the definition of actors in a network that was created by Bruno Latour and John Law. There are no hierarchies of actors in the system: every person, piece of technology and object are considered equals. What is most important is the information that is passed between them.

Entrainment

The synchronicity that occurs between people and things. It occurs when pendulums start to oscillate in rhythm. It can be seen when people start to tap their feet together in time to a beat.

SOURCES AND LINKS

Introduction

Stockton to Darlington Railway, 1825:
https://www.britannica.com/topic/Stockton-and-Darlington-Railway

Phone as an instrument of the devil:
https://www.ericsson.com/en/about-us/history/communication/
how-the-telephone-changed-the-world/the-telephone-is-the-
instrument-of-the-devil

Understanding Media, Marshall McLuhan, McGraw Hill, 1964

Interview with Nikola Tesla, *Colliers*, 1926:
http://www.tfcbooks.com/tesla/1926-01-30.htm

Interview with Bill Gates, *The Sunday Times*, April 2018:
https://www.thetimes.co.uk/article/robots-will-take-most-jobs-
predicts-bill-gates-nt9jzg2c5

1: Our brave new digital world

The New Atlantis, Francis Bacon,1627:
https://www.thomasmorestudies.org/docs/Bacon.pdf

The Tempest, William Shakespeare, 1611

Brave New World, Aldous Huxley, Chatto & Windus, 1932

231

It's Alive: The Coming Convergence of Information, Biology and Business, Stan Davis and Chris Meyer, Texere Publishing, 2003

Market caps of digital giants:
https://www.nasdaq.com/

The past and future history of the Internet, MIT, 1997:
https://groups.csail.mit.edu/ana/Publications/PubPDFs/The%20past%20and%20future%20history%20of%20the%20internet.pdf

A brief history of the Internet, Internet Society, 1997:
https://www.internetsociety.org/internet/history-internet/brief-history-internet/

19-year-old property millionaire:
https://www.independent.co.uk/news/business/young-millionaire-akshay-ruparelia-19-year-old-entrepreneur-sold-first-house-studying-a-levels-a8011126.html

SuperJam becomes a global brand: https://shop.superjam.co.uk/

Re-imagining the workforce of the future, a report by the Ludic Group, 2017: http://www.ludicgroup.com/reimagining-the-workplace-of-the-future.html

Kodak's invention of the first digital camera: https://www.kodak.com/GB/en/corp/aboutus/heritage/milestones/default.htm

The Singularity is Near: When Humans Transcend Biology, Ray Kurzweil, Viking, 2005

2: Living in a changing world

Continuous productive urban landscapes, Bohn & Viljoen Architects:
http://www.bohnandviljoen.co.uk/

The future of employment, Carl Benedikt Frey and Michael A. Osborne, 2013:
https://www.oxfordmartin.ox.ac.uk/downloads/academic/The_Future_of_Employment.pdf

Charts showing the rise of AI:
https://www.weforum.org/agenda/2017/12/charts-artificial-intelligence-ai-index/

Rise of Robotics, *Financial Times*:
https://www.ft.com/content/6e408f42-4145-11e8-803a-295c97e6fd0b

Weapons of Math Destruction, Cathy O'Neill, Allen Lane Publishers, 2016

Made Smarter Review, Professor Juergen Meier, October 2017:
https://www.gov.uk/government/publications/made-smarter-review

Continuous Productive Urban Landscapes (CPULs):
http://www.bohnandviljoen.co.uk

Knowledge acquisition, *Nature*: https://www.nature.com/articles/s41467-018-03992-5

Nudge: Improving Decisions about Health, Wealth and Happiness, Richard H Thaler and Cass R Sunstein, Yale University Press, 2008

Oculus medium: sculpt anything with digital clay:
https://www.tomshardware.com/news/oculus-medium-touch-art-program,33061.html

Frank Duffy, *The Office and the City: 12 propositions*:
https://www.pca-stream.com/public_data/download/article/1481555183/s02_6_duffy_en.pdf

Speed factory, Adidas, *Fast Company*:
https://www.fastcompany.com/3054380/the-adidas-speed-factory-
aims-to-bring-local-customization-to-manufacturing

Knitted running shoes produced in a local shop:
https://www.thememo.com/2017/03/22/knit-for-you-adidas-custom-
made-jumper-personalisation-fashion-technology/

Swarm secrets, *Nature*:
http://www.nature.com/news/2000/000706/full/news000706-11.html

The Learning Companion, Oxford Internet Institute:
https://www.oii.ox.ac.uk/research/projects/learning-companion/

Trends in Learning Report, Open University, 2017:
http://www.open.ac.uk/business/apprenticeships/blog/trends-
learning-report-2017

Three Reasons for Basic Income, Brookings Institute, 2017:
https://www.brookings.edu/blog/future-development/2017/02/15/
three-reasons-for-universal-basic-income/

Thomas Piketty, 'What society needs is not basic income but a fair
wage', *The Wire*:
https://thewire.in/uncategorised/basic-income-fair-wage-piketty

8 reasons why experiential learning is the future of learning:
https://elearningindustry.com/8-reasons-experiential-learning-
future-learning

Gamification and game-based learning
https://www.jisc.ac.uk/guides/curriculum-design-and-support-for-
online-learning/gamification

Amazing barista coffee art: https://www.youtube.com/watch?v=CZ0pF2XU0LQ

Designing and delivering 21st Century Learning Environments, Garrick Jones, 2010

http://www.ludicgroup.com/files/ludic/downloads/LudicGroup_Environments_103010.pdf

3: The activated organization

The Soul of the White Ant, Eugene Marais, 1905

Out of Control: the New Biology of Machines, Social Systems and the Economic World, Addison Wesly, Kevin Kelly, 1994

Coral reefs as complex evolving systems: www.vliz.be/imisdocs/publications/102369.pdf

The Lydian Chromatic Concept of Tonal Organization: the Art and Science of Tonal Gravity, George Russell, Concept Publishing, 1953

Kintsugi: the centuries-old craft of repairing broken pottery: https://mymodernmet.com/kintsugi-kintsukuroi/

Japanese tea ceremony: http://japanese-tea-ceremony.net/

Steve Jobs' commitment to Zen and quality: http://uk.businessinsider.com/steve-jobs-zen-meditation-buddhism-2015-1

4: The spine

Encyclopædia Britannica, first published, 1768: https://www.britannica.com/topic/Encyclopaedia-Britannica-English-language-reference-work

The Glass Bead Game, Herman Hesse, Holt, Rinehat & Winston,1931

From the Tree to the Labyrinth: Historical Studies on the Sign and the Interpretation, Umberto Eco, Harvard University Press, 2014

5: Build together

A History of Venice, John Julius Norwich, Knopf, 1982

The Architecture of Frank Lloyd Wright, William Allin Storrer, MIT Press, 1974

Squeasewear, smart clothing for people with Autistic Spectrum Disorders:
https://www.rca.ac.uk/research-innovation/innovationrca/innovationrca-start-ups/squeasewear/

The Decision Hedgehog – Case Study on Collaborative Authoring of Outcomes: Project Dreams and Reality, P. C. Humphreys and G. A. Jones, London School of Economics and Political Science:
http://www.psych.lse.ac.uk/ifip-dss/Papers/HumphreysJones.pdf

The Lunar Society:
https://www.lunarsociety.org.uk/

Things to Come, H.G. Wells, 1936: https://www.youtube.com/watch?v=atwfWEKz00U&feature=youtu.be

Great Exhibitions: London, Paris, New York, Philadelphia, 1851-1900, Jonathan Meyer, Antique Collectors' Club, 2006

The September Issue, documentary on *Vogue,* 2009:
https://www.imdb.com/title/tt1331025/

6: The organization of one

Sapiens: A Brief History of Humankind, Yuval Noah Harari, Harvill Secker, 2014

The crisis in employee engagement, a report by Gallup, 2016:
http://news.gallup.com/businessjournal/188033/worldwide-employee-engagement-crisis.aspx

Trends in employee engagement, a report by Aon, 2017:
https://insights.humancapital.aon.com/talent-rewards-and-performance/trends-in-global-employee-engagement-2017?utm_source=ceros&utm_term=engagement17

The Complete Illustrated History of the Ancient Inca Empire: A Comprehensive Encyclopedia of the Incas and Other Ancient Peoples of South America, David M. Jones, Anness Publishing, 2012

Re-imagining the workplace of the future, Ludic:
http://ludicgroup.com/reimagining-the-workplace-of-the-future.html

Lego ideas: https://ideas.lego.com

7: Add-app-ability

Ten Books of Architecture, Marcus Vitruvius Pollio:
http://academics.triton.edu/faculty/fheitzman/Vitruvius__the_Ten_Books_on_Architecture.pdf

The Empire State Building, historical timeline:
http://www.esbnyc.com/explore/historical-timeline

Operating Manual for Spaceship Earth, R. Buckminster Fuller, 1968

How to build a house in three hours, San Diego, California, 1983: https://www.youtube.com/watch?v=vTQT-9dnrr4&feature=youtu.be

Kind of Blue, Miles Davis, 1959

8: Theatres of work

Lisbon, City of the Sea: a History, Malcolm Jack, IB Tauris, 2007

Learning Environments for Collaborative Authored Outcomes: Theatres for Learning – a brief introduction, Garrick Jones Institute of Social Psychology London School of Economics and Political Science: http://www.psych.lse.ac.uk/socialpsychology/Events/2004-05/Ps404_WShop/Documents/050118_v4.pdf

9: Build beautiful things

Sagrada Familia, Gaudi, Heaven on Earth, Gijs van Hensbergen, Bloomsbury, 2017

Gaudi's model: https://goo.gl/images/rVyHB3

10: Play the game

Thomas T. Goldsmith Jr's 'cathode ray tube amusement device': https://patents.google.com/patent/US2455992A/en

Video games pull in more revenue than film and music: https://www.nasdaq.com/article/investing-in-video-games-this-industry-pulls-in-more-revenue-than-movies-music-cm634585

Playing and Reality, David Winnicott, Tavistock, 1970

Homo Ludens: A Study of the Play-Element in Culture, Johan Huizanga, Routledge & Kegan Paul, 1949

MDA: A Formal Approach to Game Design and Game Research Robin
Hunicke, Marc LeBlanc, Robert Zubek, 2004:
http://www.aaai.org/Papers/Workshops/2004/WS-04-04/WS04-04-
001.pdf?utm_source=cowlevel

11: The power of small things

Nudge: Improving Decisions about Health, Wealth and Happiness,
Richard H Thaler and Cass R Sunstein, Yale University Press, 2008

12: Targets and the mirror

*At Home in the Universe: the Search for the Laws of Self-Organization
and Complexity*, Oxford University Press, Stuart Kaufmann, 1996

A murmuration of starlings: https://www.youtube.com/
watch?v=eakKfY5aHmY&feature=youtu.be

13: Always learning

United Airways' safety film: https://www.youtube.com/watch?v=cuR-
l2qCxBc&feature=youtu.be

British Airways' safety film: https://www.youtube.com/
watch?v=RedV-KyXWO4&feature=youtu.be

*The Fifth Discipline: The Art and Practice of the Learning
Organization,* Peter Senge, Doubleday, 1990

The Adult Learner, a Neglected Species, Malcolm Shepherd
Knowles: https://files.eric.ed.gov/fulltext/ED084368.pdf

14: Meaningful alternatives

Akhenaten and the Origins of Monotheism, James K. Hoffmeier, Oxford University Press, 2015

15: Turn it on

The Gates of Paradise: Lorenzo Ghiberti's Renaissance Masterpiece, Gary M. Radke, Yale University Press, 2007

Rules for Radicals, Saul Alinsky, Random House, 1971

Governing the Commons: The Evolution of Institutions for Collective Action, Elinor Ostrom, Cambridge University Press,1990

The Tragedy of the Commons, Garrett Hardin, 1968, Science 162:1243-1248

ACKNOWLEDGEMENTS

We would like to express our gratitude to Adam Jolly for his guidance and collaboration without whom this book would not exist.

We would like to thank Mark Harden for being such a great discussion partner for many years.

We would like to thank Paul Miller for his considered and considerate review.

We would like to thank the entire Ludic team: Alex Forbes, Alex Matthews, Aliki Paolinelis, Clemens Hackl, Daniel Marquez, Dave Wilson, Deniz Fuchidzhiev, Gabriela Francke, Georg Seiler, Graeme Coultrip, Jack Pollington, Jake Holmes, Jay Lartey, Jesse Welch-Baines, Joel Cooper, John McGinty, Karol Padiasek, Louise Ashcroft, Melanie Price, Monica Vernia, Pasha Adam and Tracey Chalcraft.

We also thank all our friends and clients who have worked, laughed and cried together with us over the years, as we have brought new things to life, in particular Chris Meyer, Ella Bennett, Simon Brown, Markus Fendrich, Alan Inglis, Emilie Neff, Manuela Becker, Rachel Rose, James Prior, Marce Cancho Rosado, Sergio Martinez-Cava Camacho, Colin Sloman, Luis Rosenthal, Richard Ruttle, Andy Goodman, Gillian Secret and Juan Luis Moreno Bau.

Paul especially thanks Zsanett, Benjamin and Leanne for their love and invaluable support during the weeks and months of being immersed with him in the wonderful world of writing.

Garrick would also like to thank Zsanett, along with Patrick and Pipper Flochel, Michael Ace, Claire Bishop, Michael Craig-Martin and Francesco Manacorda for the many inspiring conversations and their generous hospitality.